Daniel Creanga

Leon Lincoln

Microeconomics
for **A Level Year 2**

Robert Nutter

Contents

Unit 1: **The role of the entrepreneur and the profit motive**

Firms

Firms are defined as business organisations where decisions are made. They are of particular interest to economists because, as business organisations, they are typically engaged in the production of goods and services. In other words, firms combine scarce resources (factors of production) in order to produce a valuable output which satisfies human needs or wants. Factors of production are classified under the headings of land (covering all natural resources), labour (human resources), capital (man made goods for use in producing further output) and enterprise (the entrepreneur who organises the other three resources). These resources are finite in quantity and hence scarce relative to infinite human needs and wants.

Profit

This is the excess of a firm's revenue over its costs. From an economic point of view, cost means the opportunity cost of the factors of production used (i.e. the value of each factor when employed in its next best use).

A money payment for a factor of production will generally be a fairly accurate reflection of its opportunity cost, because this is the minimum payment required to ensure the factor is not lost to another use (often called transfer earnings), and one would not expect a firm to pay more than necessary for a factor's services. Consider, for example, a machine available for hire. Suppose, for the sake of simplicity, that only two firms would like to hire the machine and that it will generate £400 revenue per week for firm A and £300 for firm B. If the rent rises above £300 per week, firm B will drop out of the bidding. We therefore expect firm A to hire the machine, at a rent of marginally above £300 per week. This £300 per week represents the opportunity cost of the machine, as it would generate this sum in its next best use (with firm B).

To find the full economic cost of production we must also include a sum to represent the opportunity cost of factors of production for which no money payment is made. These may be termed **imputed costs**. Consider, for example, the person who gives up a job paying £40,000 per annum in order to set up his/her own business. This £40,000 given up is a real cost of the new business, although no money changes hands to cover this cost.

Accordingly: Economic cost = money cost + imputed cost

The accountant's measure of profit takes into account only money costs such as wages, raw materials and power. Thus, his measure of profit exceeds that of the economist, i.e. when the economic profit is zero, the accounting profit is positive. This is described as a situation in which **normal profit** is made. If revenue were to fall further, it would not be sufficient to cover the opportunity costs of all factors of production. These factors would then, in the long run, move to their next best use. Normal profit, therefore, is the minimum accounting profit required to keep factors of production in their current use. Any profit over and above this level is termed abnormal profit, supernormal or economic profit. For the entrepreneur normal profit represents his/her transfer earnings and abnormal profit represents economic rent.

To summarise:

Accounting Profit = Sales Revenue − Accounting Cost (money cost)

Economic Cost = Accounting Cost (money cost) + Opportunity Cost of the factors of production (imputed cost)

Economic Profit (abnormal profit) = Sales Revenue − Economic Cost

Resources will be attracted to those activities where abnormal profits can be earned.

Question 1.1

A recruitment consultant resigns from his £50,000 per annum position in order to set up his own business. In the process of setting up the new business, he invests £60,000 of his own capital. During the first year, premises are rented for £30,000 while the only other costs are administration (£15,000) and the salaries of two junior consultants (each £25,000). Assume that in a typical year the owner of the new firm would have received £10,000 worth of bonuses in his old salaried job. The annual interest rate is 5%. The revenue of the new business in the first year is £150,000.

(a) On the basis of these figures, identify the accounting costs and economist's imputed costs of the business.

(b) Calculate and describe the profit made last year.

(c) Repeat part (b), using an interest rate of 3%.

(d) In general, what market conditions must hold for supernormal profit to be made?

(The final part of the question should only be attempted if you have studied the theory of the firm – see Section C.)

The entrepreneur

The entrepreneur is an economic agent who perceives market opportunities and assembles factors of production to exploit them in a firm. In the static, neo-classical economics of perfect competition there is no place for the entrepreneur since it is assumed that there is perfect information and freedom of entry. Following the work of Frank Knight it can be argued that the pure function of an entrepreneur is to deal with uncertainty in the dynamic, imperfect, real world in which profit is a return to uncertainty and entrepreneurship is inseparable from control of the firm in which he operates. The essence of the entrepreneur, therefore, is that he/she is alert to gaps in the market, which others do not see, and is able to raise the finance and resources required by a firm in order to exploit the market that he/she initiates. If successful he/she will make a **supernormal/abnormal** profit that will later reduce to a normal profit, as new competitors are attracted into the market. In this conception, the pure function of an entrepreneur is as a fourth factor of production. Economists have attributed other functions than risk-taking to the entrepreneur: invention; the provision of risk capital and management, for example. Though not part of the pure entrepreneurial function, which is remunerated by profit, all these functions may be embodied in the owner of a small business. His/her remuneration may be made up of rent as an owner of land, interest as a return on capital, a wage or salary for his/her management function, and therefore as a return for his/her labour, and profit as a return for his/her entrepreneurship.

Good recent examples of successful entrepreneurs include Charles Dunstone who founded Carphone Warehouse, Anita Roddick (Body Shop), Richard Branson (Virgin), Stelios Haji-Ioannou (easyJet), Martha Lane Fox (Last Minute.com), Michael O'Leary (Ryanair) and James Dyson the vacuum and washing machine inventor. Most entrepreneurs have found the going tough at times. Trevor Bayliss the inventor of the clockwork radio originally found it difficult to get financial backers for his idea, Freddie Laker's airline collapsed in the early 1980's as did Sophie Mirman's Sock Shop chain in the early 1990's. However, the most successful entrepreneurs of recent years must surely be Sergey Brin and Larry Page who founded the internet search engine 'Google'. In the ten years up to 2008 Google turned itself into the world's biggest media business acquiring YouTube in the process. Google is now branching out into other activities some more successful than others including high tech glasses and self-driving cars.

Other notable entrepreneurs in recent years are also internet related. In 1995 Pierre Omidyar and Phil Fischner founded e-Bay, and in 2004 Mark Zuckerberg founded the social networking site Facebook which was floated on the NASDAQ in 2012 at $38 per share. By 2015 Facebook's shares were at $93 and the company, with 1.2bn users, was valued at £250bn.

A recent entrepreneurial success has been Will King with his company King of Shaves. King was made redundant in the early 1990s and started work on a shaving oil product which eased the pain of shaving-something he suffered from. The company grew from strength to strength producing a range of men's

Fair trade in coffee is an example of social entrepreneurship.

toiletries. The King of Shaves brand in 2009 was stocked in approximately 30,000 stores worldwide including the United States, Japan, Australia, New Zealand, Brazil and South Africa. The company's turnover almost doubled between 2007 and 2008.

The company faced some difficult times during and after the recent financial crisis as the clean shaven approach became less fashionable along with a contractual dispute in the US with Remington. The market is still dominated by Gillette and Wilkinson Sword with King of Shaves market share in single figures. Will King resigned as Chief Executive in 2014.

One of Britain's most famous entrepreneurs of recent years, James Dyson wants a new generation of entrepreneurs who are inventors. He has warned that Britain is lagging behind its competitors in the field of invention and technology. According to Dyson "the US files 19 times more patents than us, South Korea seven times more, China nine times more – we have stopped inventing things. Pharmaceutical companies are almost the only ones left."

Other recent British success stories include the Scottish entrepreneur Michelle Mone who developed the Ultimo lingerie brand. Another potentially successful female entrepreneur is Bianca Miller who was runner up in the 2015 television series *The Apprentice*. She has launched a range of skin tone tights aimed at the ethnic minority market and Bianca used '**crowdfunding**' to raise finance to launch her product. According to the UK Crowdfunding Association "this is a way of raising finance by asking a large number of people each for a small amount of money. Crowdfunding uses the internet to talk to potentially huge numbers of potential funders. Typically, those seeking funds will set up a profile of their project on a website such as those run by our members. They can then use social media, alongside traditional networks of friends, family and work acquaintances, to raise money. There are three different types of crowdfunding: donation, debt and equity."

The government introduced the StartUp loans programme in 2012 which is targetted at 18-24 year olds who find difficulties when applying for loans from banks. Typical loans are about £5,000 with interest charged at inflation plus 3 per cent. The loan will have to be repaid in five years. It is hoped that the scheme will launch 45,000 start-ups. To date the scheme has given out 25,000 loans, created 32,000 jobs and lent £130m of the £310m provided in funding.

The government has also lent its financial support to 'peer to peer' (P2P) lending where small businesses link directly to individuals and organisations with the latter lending money to the former. This enables small

high risk ventures to have access to loan finance that would not be provided by the banks. In 2016 the government introduced the Innovative Finance ISA for P2P lenders which means that the interest paid by borrowers is tax free.

Social entrepreneurship has been more prominent since the start of the twenty-first century. The social entrepreneur runs firms that tackle social or environmental issues while also attempting to make a profit.

A social enterprise is a business that trades for a social and/or environmental purpose. It will have a clear sense of its 'social mission': which means it will know what difference it is trying to make, who it aims to help, and how it plans to do it. It will bring in most or all of its income through selling goods or services. And it will also have clear rules about what it does with its profits, reinvesting these to further the 'social mission'.

Social enterprises come in many shapes and sizes from large national and international businesses to small community based enterprises. According to Social Enterprise UK, social enterprises should:

● Have a clear social and/or environmental mission set out in their governing documents.

● Generate the majority of their income through trade.

● Reinvest the majority of their profits.

● Be autonomous of state.

● Be majority controlled in the interests of the social mission.

● Be accountable and transparent.

● A social enterprise's primary purpose is its social and/or environmental mission – it tries to maximise the amount of social good it creates balanced against its financial goals.

Government data estimates that there are approximately 70,000 social enterprises in the UK contributing £18.5 billion to the UK economy (based upon 2012 Small Business Survey, 2013) and employing almost a million people. However, many experts contest these figures. *The Big Issue*, the Eden Project and Jamie Oliver's restaurant Fifteen are examples of social enterprises. So are award-winners Divine Chocolate, a fair trade chocolate company co-owned by the cocoa farmers' cooperative KuapaKokoo in Ghana and Timewise, which connects professionals with flexible employment opportunities.   Source: Social Enterprise UK

Britain is one of the most attractive countries in which to set up a new business. Researchers at Legatum Institute rank the top ten countries in the world for entrepreneurship and opportunity with nine of the ten countries currently being European with Hong Kong making up the ten. The rankings are as follows:

1. Sweden	6. Norway
2. Denmark	7. Iceland
3. Finland	8. Netherlands
4. Switzerland	9. UK
5. Luxembourg	10. Hong Kong

This ranking may seem strange when one considers the absence of the United States and the fact that Europe particularly France, Germany, Spain and Italy, are often criticised for failing to encourage entrepreneurship. Nonetheless the study found that European countries are investing in technological infrastructure which can support innovation but on the negative side they needed to provide a more supportive environment for entrepreneurship. According to Legatum, to be a good entrepreneurial base a country needs "a strong entrepreneurial climate in which citizens can pursue new ideas and opportunities for improving their lives, leading to higher levels of income and well-being." The Legatum researchers looked at entrepreneurial environments, innovative activities and access to opportunity. Interestingly of the ten countries shown above six appear in the World Economic Forum's Global Competitiveness Index shown in the rankings below.

1. Switzerland	6. Japan
2. Singapore	7. Hong Kong
3. United States	8. Netherlands
4. Finland	9. United Kingdom
5. Germany	10. Sweden

The World Economic Forum define **competitiveness** as "the set of institutions, policies, and factors that determine the level of productivity of a country. The level of productivity, in turn, sets the level of prosperity that can be reached by an economy. The productivity level also determines the rates of return obtained by investments in an economy, which in turn are the fundamental drivers of its growth rates. In other words, a more competitive economy is one that is likely to grow faster over time."

This index is derived from twelve different measures of **competitiveness** shown below.

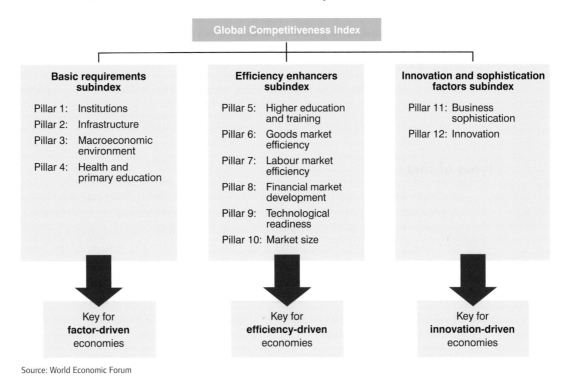

Source: World Economic Forum

Question 1.2

Read the passages on the previous pages before responding to the following:

(a) Explain the claim that the function of an entrepreneur is risk-taking.

(b) How is it that there is only a role for an entrepreneur if the market is imperfect?

(c) "Entrepreneurship is the fourth factor of production". What is meant by this statement?

(d) There has been much talk in recent years about the development of an 'enterprise culture'. Why might this be considered important?

(e) Research a well known entrepreneur. In what sense is he or she so?

Why is profit important in a free market economy?

From the preceding analysis it is clear that profit fulfils some important functions:

1. It rewards risk takers such as shareholders and entrepreneurs.

2. It provides a stimulus to innovation to introduce new products and new production techniques.

3. It provides a source of funds for investment and research and development (retained profit).

4. It sends signals to potential investors and entrepreneurs because resources are drawn towards the production of goods where profits can be earned. This helps to allocate resources efficiently.

Unit 2: **The birth and growth of firms**

Measures of the size of a firm

There are a number of ways in which we can attempt to measure the size of a firm. These include: (1) Sales turnover; (2) Numbers employed; (3) Market share; (4) Stock market value (market capitalisation); (5) The value of its assets.

It does not follow that all five measures above move in the same direction. It is important to remember that some firms may have a low value of fixed assets but a high turnover, e.g. lastminute.com, and some firms may have a relatively small number of workers but a high turnover, e.g. an oil company such as Shell.

Types of firm

In the private sector there are various types of firm as defined by their legal structure. The sole trader is a firm owned by one person who usually makes all the decisions, although there may be other people employed by the firm. The partnership is owned by between two and twenty partners who enter into a partnership agreement. Some partners play no active part in the running of the business and are called sleeping partners. Profits are shared between the partners usually in proportion to their investment. Sole traders are often small shops and partnerships and are typically found among dentists and small building firms. Both types of business have **unlimited liability** which means that the owners are liable in full for all the debts of the business, although there are some exception provisions for partners in the form of limited liability partnerships.

Shareholders in a limited company who elect a board of directors to run the business on a day-to-day basis own a limited company. The shareholders have limited liability which means that their liability for the firm's debts is limited to the amount they invested in the business. Unlike unlimited liability the shareholders cannot lose their personal possessions if the firm is placed into receivership. There are two types of limited company, **private limited** (with Ltd after their name) and **public limited** (with PLC after their name). In a private limited company shareholders cannot sell their shares without permission, thus unlike a PLC, shares are not traded openly. A PLC's shares are traded on the Stock Exchange and shareholders are free to sell their shares whenever they like in what is essentially a second hand market. The share price of quoted PLCs will rise or fall depending on the forces of demand and supply, which are operating on the Stock Market. PLCs are usually large businesses such as Marks and Spencer and British Airways. However both types of limited companies are governed by the similar rules of a joint stock company laid down in the **Articles and Memorandum of Association**. The Board of Directors of a limited company is elected by the shareholders to whom they recommend a dividend (share of the profits).

Many private limited companies are small family businesses and in some the shareholders and board members are the same people. However, there are some large private companies such as Virgin, JCB, Dyson and Arcadia (which owns Top Shop). The trend towards private company status even among larger companies is partly explained by the complex rules and regulations associated with the corporate governance of PLCs. Many well known household names are now delisted having been taken over by **private equity firms**. Private equity firms raise funds from institutional investors such as pension funds, insurance companies and wealthy individuals. They use these funds, along with borrowed money and their managerial skills to build and invest in companies that have the potential for growth. Alliance Boots was initially a British PLC *and* listed on the London Stock Exchange. In 2007 it was bought out in a private equity transaction. In 2008 the trading business was transferred to a Swiss limited company, which is a wholly owned subsidiary of a British company, AB Acquisitions Holdings Limited, which is owned by the private equity firm Kohlberg Kravis Roberts (KKR). In 2014 Boots was purchased by Walgreens who have the largest chain of retail pharmacies in the US. Boots and Walgreen became subsidiaries of Walgreen Boots Alliance.

Franchises have become increasingly popular in recent years. The franchiser has a business plan which the franchisee must follow. The franchiser who receives royalty payments from the franchisee's income often provides the premises, training, advertising and materials. There are also many non-profit making organisations such as **mutual organisations** which are found in the financial sector, mainly among building societies and life assurance businesses. **Public corporations** are trading companies which operate commercially recovering their costs from fees charged to customers. A statutory corporation is created by an Act of Parliament statute and it has no shareholders. Its powers are set out in the Act of Parliament which created it. Many public corporations, such as British Railways and the National Coal Board, were privatised in the 1980s and 90s. Channel Four Television Corporation and the Civil Aviation Authority are examples of public corporations. Slightly different public ownership structures also exist for example Network Rail is in the public sector as a central government body but is not a public corporation because 50% of its costs are not met by sales. Network Rail has huge debts which are now part of the National Debt. The government also holds shareholdings in public limited companies, for example it holds just less than an 11% stake in Lloyds Banking Group – a result of the government's rescue of the banking sector during the financial crisis in 2008-09. The government also holds a 73% stake in RBS Banking Group for the same reason. UK Financial Investments (UKFI) is a limited company set up in November 2008 and obligated by the UK Government to manage the Treasury's shareholdings in commercial banks. **Co-operatives**, which can be worker owned or customer owned (the retail Co-op), have the potential to offer a sense of belonging and unity of purpose to the owners which is not found in conventional private sector firms.

The benefits of size

Economic theory predicts that large firms are likely to enjoy significant cost advantages due to economies of scale (see Figure 2.1 and Unit 4). The large firm operates further along its long run average cost (LRAC) curve than a small firm (e.g. Point B as opposed to Point A). The calculation of short and long run costs is covered in Unit 4.

Figure 2.1: Long run costs

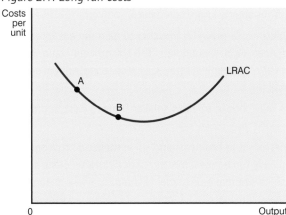

The small firm

The definition of a small firm depends largely on one's purpose; for example, if we are concerned mainly with small firms as employers, then numbers employed is important. According to the Bolton Report (1971) small firms have three distinguishing features: holding a relatively small share of the market; being managed by their owners in a personalised way, and not through any formalised management structure; not being part of any larger enterprise, so that owner-managers are free from any form of outside control. Small firms are usually sole traders, partnerships or private limited companies.

Continued existence and survival of small firms can be accounted for by the following factors:

1. The minimum efficient scale of production (the level of output at which long run average costs are minimised) is low in many industries, thus there is little or no cost disadvantage to being small. There are no significant economies of scale for such firms as they have low fixed costs, e.g. small independent plumbers, decorators, electricians, etc.

The UK has 2,400 Spar stores which turnover £3bn in retail sales a year and employ over 50,000 people.

2. Some specialist or niche markets exist that large companies do not wish to supply: Consider the demand for non-standard forms of production (e.g. in some forms of engineering and construction) or the irregular opening hours of corner shops, for instance.

3. The value placed upon personal attention in some areas, especially the service industries or the repair of products such as washing machines with parts and also advice, e.g. management consultants. The convenience of small corner shops is another factor.

4. Contracting out. Many small firms supply larger companies.

5. Co-operatives. Independent businesses may join together to gain the advantages of bulk-buying while still retaining their independence. A good example is the UK grocery chain Spar. In the UK there are 2,400 Spar stores which turnover £3.0 billion in retail sales a year and employ over 50,000 people. Many workers co-operatives are small firms.

6. Monopoly power. Large firms may choose to allow smaller firms to exist in order to disguise restrictive practices (see Unit 16).

7. Small businesses can quickly respond to problems and solve them due to a smaller chain of command. A small business can adapt quickly to changes in market conditions whereas a larger firm requires a lot of time and resources because its size makes it harder to adapt to these changes.

8. Many family businesses remain small as they wish to remain in control of their business and don't want to take the risk of expansion and diluting the ownerships of their business.

The growth of firms

There are two sources of growth. **Internal growth** refers to a straight-forward increase in a firm's output scale of production e.g. the growth of easyJet; **external growth** occurs through merger with, or acquisition of, another company (see Unit 3) e.g. Sainsbury's merger with Argos. Motivation for growth may take one of the following forms:

1. A larger company may be able to exploit economies of scale more fully.

2. A larger company will enjoy a greater degree of market power, and will therefore be better able to exploit its market.

3. If the increase in size implies more product diversity, the company may be better able to withstand downturns in the economic cycle.

4. Some firms wish to expand into new markets where there are major growth prospects.

Growth, however, sometimes brings disadvantages:

1. The potential for suffering from diseconomies of scale (see Unit 4).

2. The inability to pay customers personal attention.

3. Some companies may expand too fast as did Sock Shop in the 1980's and find that they have insufficient **working capital** to cope with the extra commitments of a larger firm such as higher interest payments and more creditors. Expansion will increase a firm's financial commitments and with insufficient working capital it can simply run out of cash. Business tends to call this problem **overtrading** and many firms have learnt to their cost that cash and profit are not the same thing and many profitable firms have gone out of business because they have run out of cash. Cobra Beer expanded rapidly a few years ago but failed to budget for a profit and was hit badly by the credit crunch in 2008. After going into administration Cobra was bought by Molson Coors in 2009.

Constraints on business growth

1. In the BBC television programme 'Dragon's Den' potential entrepreneurs pitch for investment funds from the 'Dragons'. Very often they are unsuccessful because although the product or service has a market it cannot be 'scaled up' as there is a limit to the market size and the extent to which the business can expand.

2. Many small businesses find it difficult to access finance for growth from banks as they pose too large a risk for a lender and have no assets to act as collateral security.

3. The owners and investors have to have the aspiration to grow and also the expertise and skills to push the business forward. Many small business owners do not want to take the risks this involves nor do they have the long term commitment to extensive growth.

4. Many businesses are reluctant to grow because when this happens they incur legal and administrative costs which they avoid if they stay small. For example a business does not have to register for VAT if sales revenue is below £82,000. When it employs five or more employees the business needs to have a stakeholder pension scheme in place and a formal health and safety policy.

5. It is often difficult to grow a business when within the same sector larger firms have extensive patent and copyright protection for their products.

Growth of self-employment

Figure 2.2: Change in the number of self employed, 2013-14

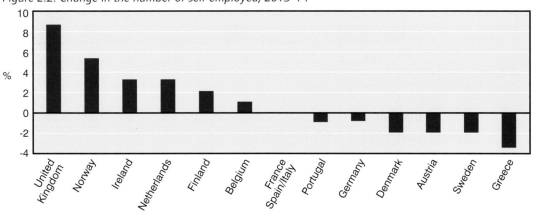

Source: Eurostat

In recent years there has been a significant growth in self-employment in the UK – now accounting for 1 in 7 of the workforce. There is increasing evidence that older workers are seeing self-employment as an alternative to retirement meaning that a growing number of experienced and skilled people remain in the workforce. Many people have also taken up self-employment because they have been unable to find a job and for some it is a tough working environment with the average income of the self-employed only £11,000 per year with no access to statutory sick pay or maternity leave. The wages of the self-employed

are not included in the official average earnings statistics and in recent years have not grown as much as salaried workers. On the positive side there are increasing numbers of young people opting to be self-employed. Often called the 'Millennials' (those in their 20s or early 30s) they are seen as far more individualistic and self-reliant than other generations such as Generation X and the much older Baby Boomers.

Figure 2.3: Self-employed as a percentage of total UK workforce

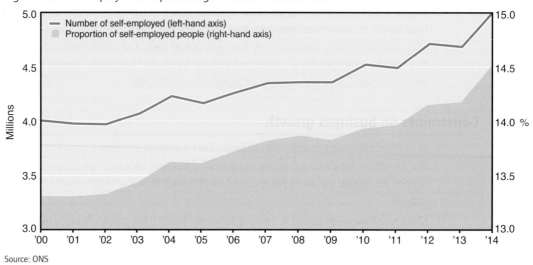

Source: ONS

Figure 2.4: Number of home workers in the UK

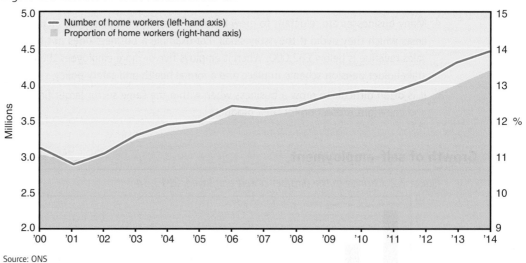

Source: ONS

Question 2.1

Research how the following help small firms:
(i)   Enterprise Finance Guarantee Scheme;   (iii) R&D tax credits;
(ii) The Prince's Trust;   (iv) National Loan Guarantee Scheme.

Question 2.2

Investigate the success of small breweries such as the Rebellion Beer Company.
http://www.rebellionbeer.co.uk/

Question 2.3

What are the functions of the British Business Bank?

Unit 3: **Forms of growth**

Types of growth

The growth of firms can be classified in terms of two categories. Internal growth refers to a firm becoming larger by expanding in its current market or finding new markets. Easyjet and Ryanair are good examples of firms that have largely grown internally. Sometimes this is called organic growth where a firm expands from its own internally generated resources. External growth refers to the integration (joining together) of two formerly separate firms. Integration can take the form of a voluntary merger or a contested takeover.

Types of integration

Horizontal: Integration between firms at the same stage of production or distribution. The merger of the ITV companies Carlton and Granada in 2003 to form ITV created a national broadcasting entity, which had once been a number of regional television companies. Although names like Meridian, Central and Anglia survive ITV is now fully horizontally integrated. The changing nature of television such as the emergence of digital broadcasting and the competition from cable and satellite channels made such a merger logical. The only concern expressed by the then competition authorities (Office of Fair Trading) over this merger was the enormous selling power ITV would have when it came to selling advertising time as it remains the biggest terrestrial commercial broadcaster in the UK. In the same vein the 2005 takeover of the cable company Telewest by its rival NTL was horizontal integration and seen as being in the public interest (the company is now known as Virgin Media). The new company cemented the fragmented cable network providers into one firm; a strong rival to BT and BSkyB. In the summer of 2005 HMV, the retail group which owned the bookseller Waterstones showed an interest in buying a fierce rival of the latter, Ottakers. The retail book market would then have been highly concentrated with 25% of the market controlled by the merged company. Both authors and publishers expressed concern that such a merger would not be in the public interest and invited the competition authorities to investigate but they cleared the takeover. In the autumn of 2005 the Office of Fair Trading (OFT) referred the horizontal acquisition of HP Foods (owned by the French company Danone) by HJ Heinz to the Competition Commission. The OFT felt that the ownership of so many brands of soup and sauces (Lee & Perrins/Daddies) by one firm could lead to higher prices. However, the Competition Commission said that the merger would not be expected to result in a substantial lessening of competition within the markets for the supply of tomato ketchup, brown sauce, barbecue sauce, tinned baked beans and tinned pasta products in the UK.

Significant horizontal mergers in recent years include the expansion of Banco Santander by purchasing Abbey National in 2004 and the savings accounts of the Bradford and Bingley Building Society and Alliance and Leicester during the credit crunch in 2008. Other notable horizontal mergers have been the supermarket takeover when Morrison's bought Safeway in 2003. More controversial was the takeover by Lloyds TSB of HBOS in 2008 which was brokered by the government during the 2008 banking crisis. In normal circumstances the OFT would never have allowed the merger due to competition issues and the 40% market share of the combined group but in that particular case the national interest was seen as more important than the public interest.

More recent horizontal mergers include the creation of International Airlines Group (IAG) in 2011 when British Airways merged with the Spanish national carrier Iberia. In 2012 IAG bought BMI from Lufthansa and in 2013 purchased the Spanish budget airline Vueling. Most recently Aer Lingus became part of the IAG group in 2015. Established airlines facing challenges from large budget carriers such as Ryanair and easyJet have used horizontal mergers as the way to develop a lower cost base.

Also in 2015 betting firms Ladbrokes and Gala Coral announced that they intended to merge to create a £2.3bn gambling giant. With nearly 4,000 betting shops and 30,000 employees, the combined group is set to overtake William Hill as Britain's biggest bookmaker. Similar mergers are likely to occur in the gambling

sector as firms face the challenge of the increased popularity of online gambling often via mobile phones and tablets.

Note: Since 2014 the Office of Fair Trading and the Competition Commission have been replaced by the Competition and Markets Authority (see Unit 16).

Vertical: Integration between firms at different stages of production or distribution. If the firm taken over is at the next stage of the production or distribution process (e.g. a brewery buying a chain of pubs), then the integration is known as **forward-vertical**. A brewery buying a hops farm, on the other hand, is an example of **backward-vertical** integration. Vertical integration is common in the media. News Corporation owns 20th Century Fox and the latter's film library provides a source for the many movie channels operated by Sky and other TV channels owned by the company. Since 2004 Sony has owned MGM which has 4,000 films in its library. Sony can use these films for video on demand and cable channels. While the latter are examples of backward vertical integration some businesses are fully vertically integrated forwards and backwards. For example BP as well as refining crude oil into petrol is also engaged in oil exploration and distribution of petrol at its filling stations. In October 2005 the Indian firm Apeejay Surrendra Group bought Typhoo tea from Premier Foods for £80m. Apeejay Surrendra grow a lot of tea in their Indian plantations, and buying Typhoo who blend and package tea should result in the benefits of forward vertical integration.

Vertical integration has occurred in the UK energy market where the so-called 'Big Six' companies dominate not just the wholesale market (generating energy) but also the retail side (supplying it to consumers). The 'Big Six' generate 70 per cent of the energy used in the UK and supply over 90 per cent of households. The companies defend the integration that they have created, largely by merger, saying that combining generation and supply helps to deliver the secure energy supplies that customers demand. However, smaller energy suppliers have complained about the substantial barriers to entry in the industry. In particular, they normally have to buy wholesale from one of the Big Six. Lack of transparency concerning their costs and internal transfer prices has led to suspicions that the Big Six are charging more to independent suppliers than to themselves. Nonetheless smaller suppliers have begun to make inroads into the market and large scale redundancies at Npower in March 2016 are signs of a change to the dominance of the 'Big Six'. The 'Big Six' now have to sell 25% of their generated power on the open market to encourage the expansion of small independent suppliers who don't generate their own electricity.

Conglomerate: Integration between firms that are in different, unrelated industries. These firms are said to be diversified. Conglomerate mergers are less common than they were in the 1960's and 1970's. Many large diversified conglomerates that grew through acquisition have been slimmed down in recent years to concentrate on core activities. For example Lonrho, which was once a huge conglomerate, was demerged in 1998 into Lonrho (focusing on hotels, property and distribution) and Lonmin, a mining company. In addition Hanson Trust split into four separate companies in 1996 (see the section on demergers). The era of the great industrial conglomerate seemed to have disappeared in the new century but the Indian giant Tata Group is a good modern day example. It operates in 80 countries and is involved in seven different sectors which include steel, tea, hotels, construction and cars (it owns Jaguar and Land Rover). Similarly the Apeejay Surrendra Group is involved in tea production, shipping, hotels and financial services.

Lateral: Integration between firms that are in different but related industries. The acquisition of Gillette by Procter and Gamble in 2004 is a good example of a lateral merger of two firms selling household consumer goods. Procter and Gamble is the biggest brands company owning Daz, Bold, Crest, Max Factor and Pampers. Gillette, apart from razors, owns Duracell batteries, Oral-B toothbrushes and Right Guard deodorant. In 2008 the Mars takeover of Wrigley was also a lateral merger with chocolate and chewing gum both being in the confectionery market. In 2010 the Kraft takeover of Cadbury was an example of a lateral merger as both companies made a variety of similar products in the food and drinks sector. Lateral mergers can be particularly beneficial in that they provide opportunities for **economies of scope** (see Unit 4).

This can be seen when Currys and PC World owner Dixons merged with mobile phone retailer Carphone Warehouse in 2014 to form Dixons Carphone. For the two companies this merger is all about looking to the future and the word 'connectivity'. Dixons and Carphone Warehouse claim they are preparing for the 'internet of things', where household appliances are all connected to the internet. Thus phones sold by Carphone will link to microwaves sold in Currys. Sebastian James, of Dixons, has said that the number of items connected to the internet in our homes will rise from four to more than 20 in the next few years. This will include fridges that send emails and order replacements when food is going off and security systems that text smartphones when they detect suspicious activities in the house. Your mobile phone will thus be able to switch off the cooker! Unfortunately, according to collated research and a recent Harvard Business Review Report, the failure rate of mergers and acquisitions is between 70% and 90%.

In recent years it has become popular for firms to co-operate in **alliances** and **joint ventures**. In the airline industry Star Alliance, One World and SkyTeam are three groups of airlines which are integrated worldwide as air transport networks. Globalisation, increased airline competition and changes in passenger demands for air travel have meant that a single airline cannot sustain and respond alone to these changes. When two or more firms, enter into an agreement to combine resources for a specific business undertaking, it is referred to as a **joint venture**. The organisation of a joint venture serves as a short term partnership for the duration of the project, in which each participant shares responsibility for the project's associated costs, profits, and losses. In recent years these arrangements have been common in the car industry particularly between car manufacturers in the west and Chinese firms. China has surpassed the United States as the world's biggest car market. In 2013 sales of domestically made cars reached 16 million and two thirds of these were foreign models manufactured by Chinese joint ventures. Some of the top Chinese automotive companies are almost entirely dependent on selling overseas brands. For the Shanghai Automotive Corporation 89% of the passenger cars it sold in 2013 were from joint ventures with General Motors and Volkswagen. Virgin Mobile India Limited is a cellular telephone service provider company which is a joint venture between Tata Tele service and Richard Branson's Service Group. Currently, the company uses Tata's CDMA network to offer its services under the brand name Virgin Mobile.

Market concentration

The extent to which a small group of firms controls a given percentage of output or sales can be measured by the use of a **concentration ratio**. A simple concentration measure for a particular industry could be a '4 firm concentration ratio of 85%'. This means that the four largest firms in an industry account for 85% of the total output. Horizontal mergers tend to increase market concentration. Markets with a high level of concentration often give increased market power to the largest firms with some control over price. Highly concentrated markets are often called **oligopolies** (see Unit 10).

The data below refers to the market shares of the major film studios. There is a four firm concentration ratio of 64.7% because the four largest firms account for 64.7% of sales. An alternative measure of market concentration is the **Herfindahl Index**. It is often seen as more accurate than the simple concentration ratio because it considers all the firms in a market rather than just the largest. The index is calculated by squaring the percentage market share of each firm in the market and summing these numbers. The index can be as high as 10,000 for a pure monopoly with a 100% market share to as little as 10 or less for perfect competition.

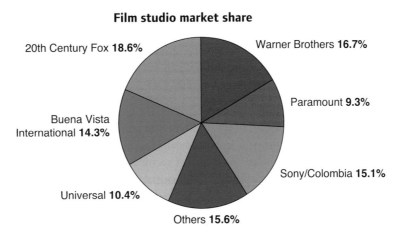

Film studio market share

20th Century Fox **18.6%**
Warner Brothers **16.7%**
Paramount **9.3%**
Buena Vista International **14.3%**
Sony/Colombia **15.1%**
Universal **10.4%**
Others **15.6%**

Some markets have a fairly low level of concentration, for example women's clothing. The womenswear market is very competitive and in recent years traditional mass market retailers such as C&A and Littlewoods

have been replaced by more dynamic value-led retailers such as Primark, Matalan and TK Maxx. A major highlight is Primark's continued encroachment on the Arcadia brands such as Topshop, Miss Selfridge and Wallis. The market leader, M&S, continues to lose market share – a trend which the company to date have failed to reverse. Another victim of changing times is British Home Stores which after mounting losses was sold by Arcadia for £1 to Retail Acquisitions Ltd, but in 2016 went into administration.

Womenswear market, share by value

	2012 (est.)
Marks & Spencer	11.2%
Arcadia Group	8.1%
Next	6.9%
Primark	6.2%
New Look	3.3%
Asda	3.2%
Debenhams	2.9%
Topshop	2.8%
TK Maxx	2.8%
Matalan	2.7%
H&M	2.5%

Source: Verdict

The implications of growth

External growth has a number of attractions for the firm:

1. Rapid growth and acquisition of market power. Integration offers possibilities of increased market share and acquisition of valuable brand names. In recent years it has become common for a sum representing the value of a brand name to be included as an asset in the balance sheets of firms, even though this is an intangible asset. Acquiring brand names and market share through integration may prove cheaper, and is certainly quicker, than the alternative of internal growth.

2. Economies of scale. Expansion of output in the case of horizontal integration offers potential for lower long run average costs from a wide range of sources (technical, managerial, commercial, financial and risk-bearing economies of scale). For example the horizontal mergers that have produced Glaxo SmithKline Beecham (GSK) has given the firm significant research economies of scale in the pharmaceuticals sector. In the case of vertical integration, cost savings are made through cutting out profit margins at intermediate stages of production. A brewery, for example, that purchased a hops farm would now receive cheaper supplies of that particular ingredient and have greater control over quality of inputs. Vertical integration also can act as a barrier to entry making markets less contestable. Firms which are vertically integrated backwards or forwards can deny potential or new entrants access to supplies of raw materials and selling outlets.

3. Diversification. Conglomerate and lateral integration take firms into different product areas, making them better able to withstand a slump in any one market, while horizontal integration can give more geographical or brand diversification.

Integration is not always a success, however. The potential for **diseconomies of scale** should be considered and many of the mergers of the 1980s proved unsuccessful as measured by post merger profitability, with the profit made by the new, larger company falling short of the combined profits of the previously separate firms. More recently in the supermarket sector when Morrisons took over Safeway in 2003 there was not perfect synergy as management and financial cultures differed between the two firms. Some companies have resorted to demerging in order to improve performance. One of the best recent examples of a failed merger was Daimler-Chrysler. Daimler-Benz bought Chrysler for $36bn in 1998 but the 'marriage' never worked chiefly because the cultures of the two car manufacturing firms were so different at management level. After nine years Daimler sold Chrysler to Cerberus, a private equity group. Dieter Zetsche, a senior Daimler executive, said of the ill-fated merger, "we overestimated the potential of synergies".

From an economy's point of view, integration is often regarded as detrimental:

1. It can confer a degree of **monopoly power**, which the neo-classical structure-conduct-performance model (see Unit 8) suggests will lead to the exploitation of the consumer.

2. Post merger rationalisation often leads to a direct loss of jobs (the Leeds-Halifax merger in 1995, for example, resulted in the closure of some branches, particularly where the two societies had branches in close proximity). Similar job losses followed the emergency banking mergers of 2008 as a result of the credit crunch. In June 2009 Lloyds announced the closure of its Cheltenham and Gloucester Building Society branches.

The economist Geoffrey Meeks undertook a detailed analysis of over 1,000 mergers in the UK post-World War Two period and found that in general mergers led to a decline in the profitability of the companies involved and certainly didn't result in any increase. Very often there is an overestimation of the synergies a merger will yield. These synergies can come from economies of scale and scope, best practice, the sharing of capabilities and opportunities, and, often, the stimulating effect of the merger on the individual companies. However, it takes only a very small degree of error in estimating these values to cause an acquisition or a merger to fail to meet expectations.

Microsoft bought Nokia for $9.4 billion in April 2014 and at the time the then-CEO of Microsoft Steve Ballmer was quoted as saying "together as one company with the devices folks at Nokia, we'll do a phenomenal job." However just over a year later, their CEO Satya Nadella announced that it is writing down almost the entire value of Nokia handset acquisition and announcing sweeping job cuts. Microsoft's attempts to use the purchase of Nokia to challenge the market dominance of Apple and Google in smartphone software had failed.

It has been suggested that a year after the merger fewer than 3 per cent of new smartphones were running Windows. The cost of the asset write down was huge. Microsoft said it would take a write-down of $7.6bn related to the Nokia acquisition and there was a restructuring charge of $750m-$850m, including the cost of redundancies – over 7,500 people.

Despite this, integration can sometimes receive government encouragement, because domestic firms may need to be large to compete internationally. Sometimes a merger may be encouraged by the government because it is in the public or national interest. The Lloyds Bank takeover of HBOS in 2009 was pushed through by the then Labour Chancellor Alistair Darling as a means of stopping HBOS from collapsing. Competition rules were ignored for it to go ahead. In the end the government had to bail out the newly merged Lloyds bank and take part ownership of it. However, internal growth is generally held in more favourable regard than external growth. This is especially so when it entails product innovation such as has been seen with Dyson's vacuum cleaners and hand dryers. Marks and Spencer and more recently Virgin have grown through internal growth whereas easyJet has grown by both internal and external growth. Easyjet has grown in size in the low cost airline market by its own success and by taking over one of its rivals, the British Airways subsidiary, 'Go', some years ago.

Easyjet has grown by both internal and external growth.

The trend towards demerger

Demerging is the process of disposing of part of an organisation by selling it. Since the 1990's a trend towards the break-up of larger companies began to emerge. It appeared that difficulties inherent in managing large firms, particularly conglomerates, were being recognised and that many companies saw the benefits in becoming 'more focused' on particular lines of business. Typical of this trend were the selling off of some Forte assets after the group had been taken over by Granada and the splitting of the Hanson conglomerate into four separate firms announced in February 1996. In the same month, British Gas announced that it would split into two companies, one responsible for the maintenance of the pipe network (Transco) and the other for gas supply (Centrica). This move was made in response to the forthcoming removal of the company's monopoly over domestic gas supply. ICI demerged part of its group into Zeneca in 1993, and in 2001 BT demerged into BT Group and O₂. It is possible that failed mergers can subsequently lead to demergers. Cadbury grew over the years as a food and drinks business but in more recent years changed direction. With the disposal of Schweppes and Dr. Pepper in 2007, Cadbury focussed on its confectionery – mainly chocolate.

The Chairman at the time, Sir John Sunderland, praised the Cadbury Schweppes' demerger into confectionery and beverages in March 2007:

> "We believe now is the moment to separate and give both management teams the focused opportunity to extract the full potential inherent in these excellent businesses."

However, in 2009 Cadbury itself was controversially taken over by the US food giant Kraft and then in 2011 the enlarged company was demerged with Kraft chairman and chief executive Irene Rosenfeld justifying the plan to split up as follows:

> "Our strategic actions have put us in a position to create two great companies, each with the leadership, resources and strong market positions to realize their full potential."

The main motives for demergers focus on several issues. Sometimes the problems of **diseconomies of scale** – mainly managerial – are the main factor. In addition changes in market conditions are important with the result that the firm reassesses its strategic direction. Technological change can also play a part with new markets developing and others declining. The demerger of Cable and Wireless in 2010 was motivated in part by the explosive demand for telecoms bandwidth across the globe. Clearly pressures from shareholders, who are always looking for increases in shareholder value, are also an important factor in decisions on whether to demerge. This quote from Cable and Wireless plc illustrates this point:

> "In November 2009, Cable and Wireless plc announced its intention to separate Communications and Worldwide, reflecting the Board's belief that the two businesses had reached a position where they are best placed to deliver further value to shareholders as separately listed companies."

Common reasons for demerging are a company's desire to focus on its core activities and dispose of what it calls peripheral activities. Often demergers result from part of the company persistently underperforming or because the anticipated benefits of a merger have failed to materialise. Companies may not have the resources or expertise in a market that is becoming more challenging due to technological change or facing major changes in market conditions.

Anecdotal evidence suggests that the share prices of recently demerged companies move favourably post-demerger with increased rates of return and higher shareholder value. With regard to organisational restructuring many demerged firms tend to develop flatter organisational charts. In search of efficiencies, some of them remove entire layers of management to speed up communication and reduce the number of employees. Evidence from recent demergers seems to suggest that a split in a business can be organisationally disruptive as it can cause stress and a breakdown of trust between employees who feel insecure and no longer in control of their careers. In 2015 Hewlett Packard (HP) split into two businesses HP Inc. and HP Enterprise. HP Inc. will comprise the company's computer and printer businesses whilst Hewlett-Packard Enterprise will consist of the company's technology infrastructure, software and services businesses. It is possible that the demerger will lead to job losses of 55,000 employees globally. Even for those workers not affected by redundancy there will be reorganisations which are often unsettling and will take time to bed in.

The Clydesdale and Yorkshire banking group, currently owned by National Australia Bank (NAB), is planning a major investment in new IT after it demerged in 2015. The demerged business has plans to invest in more digital developments, according to an announcement by Debbie Crosbie, acting CEO of the newly created banking group who said; "Support for customers will continue to be at the heart of our business." In theory demerged companies should be able to focus better on their customers once they are free to make their own decisions rather than conform to a larger firm's corporate strategy that doesn't fit their aims and objectives.

One of the most significant demergers in recent years concerned Kraft Foods which demerged its company in 2012 only two years after buying Cadbury. The passage which follows is how the demerger was justified by Kraft.

Kraft demerger announced

Kraft Foods Inc today announced that its Board of Directors intends to create two independent public companies: A high-growth global snacks business with estimated revenue of approximately $32 billion and a high-margin North American grocery business with estimated revenue of approximately $16 billion. The company expects to create these companies through a tax-free spin-off of the North American grocery business to Kraft Foods shareholders.

"As our second quarter results once again show, our businesses are benefiting from a virtuous cycle of growth and investment, which we fully expect will continue," said Chairman and CEO Irene Rosenfeld. "We have built two strong, but distinct, portfolios. Our strategic actions have put us in a position to create two great companies, each with the leadership, resources and strong market positions to realize their full potential. The next phase of our development recognizes the distinct priorities within our portfolio. The global snacks business has tremendous opportunities for growth as consumer demand for snacks increases around the world. The North American grocery business has a remarkable set of iconic brands, industry-leading margins, and the clear ability to generate significant cash flow."

Strategic rationale

Over the last several years, Kraft Foods has transformed its portfolio by expanding geographically and by building its presence in the fast-growing snacking category. A series of strategic acquisitions, notably of LU biscuits from Danone and of Cadbury Plc, together with the strong organic growth of its Power Brands, have made Kraft Foods the world's leading snacks company. At the same time, the company has continued to invest in product quality, marketing and innovation behind its iconic North American brands, while implementing a series of cost management initiatives. As a result, the company has delivered strong results in very challenging economic conditions.

Having successfully executed its transformation plan, and 18 months into the Cadbury integration, the company has, in fact, built a global snacking platform and a North American grocery business that now differ in their future strategic priorities, growth profiles and operational focus. For example, Kraft Foods' snacks business is focused largely on capitalising on global consumer snacking trends, building its strength in fast-growing developing markets and in instant consumption channels; the North

Kraft has delivered strong results in very challenging economic conditions.

American grocery business is investing to grow revenue in line with its categories in traditional grocery channels through product innovation and world-class marketing, while driving superior margins and cash flows.

Over the course of Kraft Foods' strategic transformation, the Board of Directors and management have continually explored opportunities to further enhance performance and increase long-term shareholder value and believe that creating two independent public companies is the logical next step. Specifically, detailed review by the Board and management has shown that these two businesses would now benefit from being run independently of each other, rather than as part of the same company.

The company believes that creating two public companies would offer a number of opportunities:

● Each business would focus on its distinct strategic priorities, with financial targets that best fit its own markets and unique opportunities.

● Each would be able to allocate resources and deploy capital in a manner consistent with its strategic priorities in order to optimise total returns to shareholders.

● Investors would be able to value the two companies based on their particular operational and financial characteristics and thus invest accordingly.

Creating two great companies

Global snacks will consist of the current Kraft Foods Europe and Developing Markets units as well as the North American snacks and confectionery businesses. As an independent company, global snacks would have estimated revenues of approximately $32 billion and a strong growth profile across numerous fast-growing, attractive markets. Approximately 75% of revenues would be from snacks around the world, and approximately 42% would come from developing markets, including a diversified presence in numerous highly attractive emerging markets. The business would have a strong presence in the fast-growing and high-margin instant consumption channel. The non-snacks portion of the portfolio would consist primarily of powdered beverages and coffee, which have a strong growth and margin profile in developing markets and Europe. Key brands would include *Oreo* and *LU biscuits*, *Cadbury* and *Milka* chocolates, *Trident* gum, *Jacobs* coffee, and *Tang* powdered beverages.

The North American grocery business would consist of the current US Beverages, Cheese, Convenient Meals and Grocery segments and the non-snack categories in Canada and Food Service. With approximately $16 billion in estimated revenue, this business would be one of the largest food and beverage companies in North America. Its portfolio would include many of the most popular food brands on the continent, with leadership positions in virtually every category in which it competes.

The North American grocery business would have a highly competitive retail presence, cost leadership and a continued commitment to innovation and marketing excellence. North America's strategic priorities would be to build on its leading market positions by growing in line with its categories while maintaining a sharp focus on its cost structure. Capitalising on the investments that the company has made during its transformation, an independent North American business would be managed to deliver reliable revenue growth; strong margins and free cash flow; and a highly competitive dividend payout. Key brands would include *Kraft* macaroni and cheese, *Oscar Mayer* meats, *Philadelphia* cream cheese, *Maxwell House* coffee, *Capri Sun* beverages, *Jell-O* desserts and *Miracle Whip* salad dressing.

Kraft Foods Group	Mondelez International
Kraft Cheese (Dairylea)	Cadbury (Dairy Milk)
Honey Maid	Milka
Maxwell House	Oreo
Capri Sun	Lu
Jello-O	Trident
Oscar Mayer	Tang
Miracle Whip	Toblerone

Source: Kraft Foods website: http://www.kraftfoodscompany.com

In 2015 Kraft Foods merged with HJ Heinz to form the Kraft Heinz Company. The company justified the merger as follows:

> "The transaction creates the third-largest food and beverage company in North America and the fifth-largest food and beverage company in the world with an unparalleled portfolio of iconic brands. The complementary nature of the two brand portfolios presents substantial opportunity for synergies, which will result in increased investments in marketing and innovation. This historic transaction unites two powerful businesses and iconic brands, and provides a platform for leadership in the food industry both domestically and internationally."

The new company unites Kraft's namesake cheese, Jell-O and Planters peanuts with Heinz's ketchup, baked beans and Classico sauces.

Question 3.1

In September 2015 the Competition and Markets Authority (CMA) cleared Poundland's £55m takeover of its rival single-price retailer, 99p Stores, arguing that there are enough value chains vying for customers to allow the deal to be completed. The regulator declared that there will still be plenty of choice and no threat to competition and quality if the takeover goes ahead. The acquisition of 99p Stores will add 250 extra shops to Poundland's 600 UK outlets. Discounters such as Poundland are able to sell their goods so cheaply for three key reasons. Their products are all non-perishable so they can buy in bulk. Secondly they buy directly from suppliers rather than distributors. Thirdly they work on very small profit margins on each item. However, the 99p Stores will be rebranded as Poundland, meaning regular shoppers at the acquired business will have to pay a penny more per item!

Question: Using the above information examine the reasons for Poundland's takeover of 99p Stores.

Question 3.2

Demerger survival

Peter Bartram, Financial Director, 26 April 2007

Demergers are a massive undertaking, definitely not for the faint-hearted Finance Director (FD). But done properly they can improve business focus and create long-term value. Bryan Hucker, finance director of Coda, the accounting software supplier, still bears the scars of the company's 2006 demerger from AIM-listed CodaSciSys.

"I was talking to analysts recently," he recalls. "I told them that if an FD tells them they've been through a demerger and knows everything about it, ask them one question: would you like to do another. Those who really understand it will be the ones heading for the door before you've even finished speaking."

He adds, "It was a massive exercise, beyond the understanding of anyone who has never done it." Yet, if the trend towards demergers continues to grow, more FDs could find themselves wanting to head for the door.

"Normally, you find demergers follow on after waves of substantial and sustained merger and acquisition activity," says Dr Duncan Angwin an associate professor in the strategic management group at Warwick Business School. "Sometimes, companies expand beyond their ability to control and co-ordinate. Then, perhaps, they find that they're not realising the benefits they originally anticipated," he says.

According to Thomson Financial, there were €1.35 trillion of mergers and acquisitions in Europe last year. So, if Angwin is right, FDs should brace themselves for the demerger fall-out in the next few years. Demergers have grabbed the headlines in recent weeks because of Cadbury Schweppes's

stated intention to separate its confectionery and American beverages businesses. According to chief executive Todd Stitzer, the move will enable the demerged companies "to focus on generating further revenue growth, increasing margin and enhancing returns for their respective share owners."

As Stitzer and his management team have set out a reasonably convincing strategic rationale for the demerger, he may well be right. New research suggests that companies that demerge to improve business focus as well as communication with investors are more likely to create value in the long run.

Question: What are the potential advantages and disadvantages of demergers?

Source: Financial Director

Question 3.3

What type of integration were the following mergers: Paddy Power/Betfair and Sainsbury/Argos (Home Retail Group)?

Question 3.4

The history of Santander in the UK

Since its entry into the UK market in November 2004, Santander has transformed the three businesses it acquired. The integration of separate management structures, systems and brands improved profitability and allowed Santander to broaden its range of value-for-money products which contributed to strong organic growth.

Key dates for Santander in the UK include:

● In November 2004, the courts approved Santander acquisition of Abbey National plc and Abbey became part of the Santander Group.

● In September 2008, Santander acquired Bradford & Bingley's retail branches and savings business.

● In October 2008, Santander acquired Alliance & Leicester. In January 2010, Abbey and the branch network of Bradford & Bingley rebranded as Santander.

● In August 2010, Santander agreed to purchase the parts of the banking businesses of the Royal Bank of Scotland which are carried out through its RBS branches in England and Wales, and by its NatWest branches in Scotland.

● In November 2010, Alliance & Leicester was rebranded as Santander.

Source: http://www.aboutsantander.co.uk

Question: How could Santander benefit from these acquisitions?

Short run costs

Economists distinguish between two different time periods – the short-run and the long-run – when considering costs of production. The **short-run** is defined as a period in which the enterprise has decided its 'scale of plant' (or 'capacity size') and thus can only increase output by increasing the use of that fixed capacity and by acquiring the use of additional variable factors of production, e.g. labour, raw materials. There is at least one fixed factor of production. Thus, the enterprise has some fixed costs that cannot be avoided (even if the firm stopped production) and some variable costs which are avoidable, i.e. they are directly related to output, and could be avoided if the firm closed down. Therefore, to produce any given level of output, the enterprise incurs fixed and variable costs. The fixed costs would not vary as output varies (e.g. rent, interest charges on borrowed capital, business rates and certain administration costs). Variable costs would be items such as wages (labour), raw material costs, heating, lighting, power, fuel and transport costs because they rise in total as output rises.

For any level of output, there are thus several measures of cost – this is why the expression 'cost of production' is ambiguous. Examples of costs are:

Total cost of production = Fixed costs + Variable costs

Average total cost (or per unit cost) (sometimes called 'average cost') $= \dfrac{\text{Total cost}}{\text{Output}}$

Marginal cost = The addition to total cost of producing one more unit of output

Average fixed costs $= \dfrac{\text{Total fixed cost}}{\text{Output}}$

Average variable costs $= \dfrac{\text{Total variable costs}}{\text{Output}}$

Figure 4.1: Costs in the short run

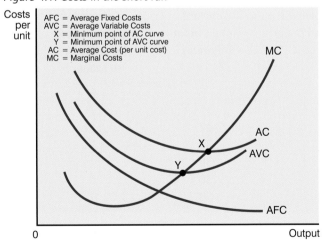

The relationship between marginal cost and average cost is essentially mathematical. If marginal cost is less than average cost, average cost is falling because the average is being pulled down. Similarly if marginal cost is greater than average cost, average cost is rising because the average is being pulled up. It is best explained in cricketing terms. When a batsman's next (marginal) innings is less than his present average the result is that the average is pulled down. The reverse occurs when the next innings is above the current average.

The marginal cost curve will therefore normally intersect the average variable cost and average cost curves from below at their lowest point.

It is important to remember that even if marginal cost is falling total costs will still be rising as long as marginal cost is positive. The basis of costs in the short-run rests on the **law of increasing/diminishing returns** to a variable factor of production, usually labour. The shapes of the marginal cost and average variable cost curves are based on increasing returns (falling marginal and average variable costs) and diminishing returns (rising marginal and average variable costs). The average cost curve will fall when both average fixed cost and average variable cost are falling. Average cost will still fall even when average variable cost is rising as long as the increase is less than the fall in average fixed costs, but it will rise when the fall in average fixed cost is less than the rise in average variable cost.

Diminishing returns should not be confused with diseconomies of scale, which is a long run concept. The diminishing returns theory relates to the additional returns (output) that result from marginal increases in a variable factor of production (e.g. labour) when it is combined with some other fixed factor of production (e.g. land or capital), which is fixed. It is essentially a relationship between input factors in the short-run whereas returns to scale is a concept which analyses what happens when all factor inputs rise.

For example, suppose additional workers (labour) are added to a fixed plot of land. Although (initially) marginal output (i.e. extra output) may increase because of teamwork; ultimately, as more and more workers are added to the fixed plot, the marginal additions will begin to diminish. The scope for increasing output when capital and land are fixed falls. In this context, if marginal returns (or product) are changing, so will average returns (or average product). Taking the example of additional workers applied to a given plot of land, one worker working the plot can produce a total output of 5 tonnes of potatoes. Two workers working the plot can produce a total of 15 tonnes of potatoes, because (a) more of the plot can be cultivated, i.e. the fixed factor is being more effectively utilised and, (b) two workers are likely to be more efficient, working as a team and dividing the work load. If the total output of the two workers is 15 tonnes, the **marginal product** (or return) of the second worker must be 10 (tonnes), i.e. his addition to total output. **Average product** rises from 5.0 to 7.5. It is not that the second worker is more efficient than the first, simply that the two workers make better use of the fixed factor. As more workers are added, total output will rise but, ultimately, the fixed factor (the plot of land) will become overworked. In this case, the marginal product (returns) of additional workers will start to diminish. Total output increases, but each time by smaller and smaller amounts. Figure 4.2 illustrates these situations and is derived from the table below.

Column 1 Number of Workers	Column 2 Fixed Factor Land	Column 3 Total Output of Potatoes	Column 4 Marginal Return (or product) to Labour	Column 5 (= Col. 3 ÷ Col. 1) Average Return (or product) to Labour
1	1	5	5	5.0
2	1	15	10	7.5
3	1	27	12	9.0
4	1	32	5	8.0
5	1	36	4	7.2
6	1	38	2	6.3
7	1	38	0	5.4

In the example, the maximum average return to labour (maximum output per worker) is achieved when three workers are applied to the fixed factor. This is referred to as the **optimum factor combination** (of fixed and variable factors). In this case, it is 1:3. It represents the best combination of fixed and variable factors in terms of output per worker, but note the total output of 32 may not be the most profitable level of output. This will depend on sales and the price of potatoes in the market. The marginal product/average product curves tell us little about profitable levels of production. The average product and marginal product curves help to determine the average cost and marginal cost curves for a firm in the short run. The relationship between the four is shown below in Figure 4.3.

Figure 4.2: Short-run returns to labour

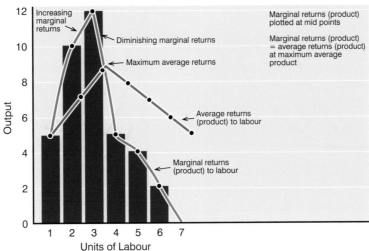

Figure 4.3: Relationship between cost and product curves

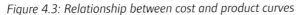

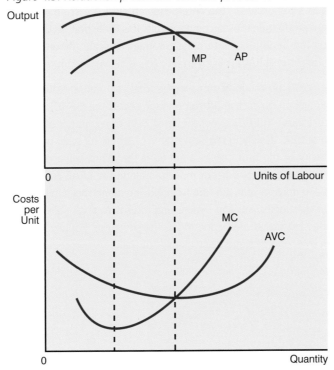

Marginal product cuts average product at its maximum point. The minimum point on the marginal cost curve is associated with the highest point on the marginal product curve. The minimum point on the average variable curve is associated with the highest point on the average product curve.

Shifts in cost curves

If there is a change in fixed costs this will shift the average cost curve. For example Figure 4.4 shows a rise in fixed costs shifting the average cost curve to the left (or upwards) from AC to AC1. Note that the marginal cost curve and obviously the average variable cost curve do not shift. Marginal costs are composed of variable costs.

If there is a change in variable costs the average cost and marginal cost curves will shift position. Thus a rise in variable costs will shift the average cost and marginal cost curves to the left (or upwards) to AC1 and MC1 as shown in Figure 4.5.

Figure 4.4

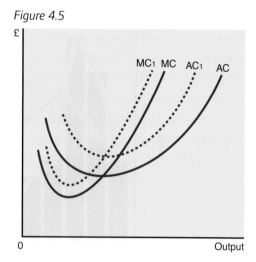

Figure 4.5

Long run costs

The long-run is defined as a period when the enterprise can alter the scale of plant (either expand or contract size). All factors of production thus become variable. It is likely that, as the scale of plant increases, the enterprise may enjoy the benefits of internal economies of scale. Where these are achieved, the average total cost in the long-run (LRAC) is likely to fall. This is shown in Figure 4.6.

Points A, B, C, represent points on the long-run average total cost curve. Note these do not necessarily correspond to the minimum point on each short-run average cost curve (SRAC), e.g. point X. All points on the long-run average cost curve (LRAC) show the least cost or minimum attainable average cost of production for any given output, assuming the firm is able to adjust its scale of plant accordingly. In the basic micro-economic theory of the firm, the assumption is that firms will always choose the least-cost method of production in the long-run and hence move out along the LRAC curve if this is possible, (lack of finance or lack of demand may prevent the firm from moving along this curve as it would like to do). It is important to remember that increasing and diminishing returns to a variable factor (e.g. labour) is the most important factor affecting the AC, AVC, and MC in the short-run. Equally the long-run average cost curve is strongly affected by economies and diseconomies of scale.

Figure 4.6: Costs in the long run

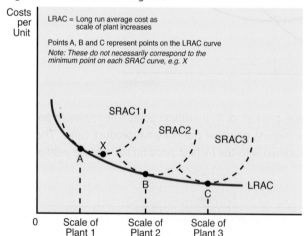

When an increase in the input of all factors of production leads to a *more than proportional* increase in output, we say that the firm has experienced **increasing returns to scale**. For example, if the firm increases the scale of production, that is the input of all factors of production, by 10 per cent, and as a result output rises by more than 10 per cent, the firm has experienced economies of scale resulting from a rise in productivity. On the other hand, when an increase in the input of all factors of production leads to a *less than proportional* increase in total output, we say that the firm experiences **decreasing returns to scale**. Thus if the firm increases the scale of production by 10 per cent and output rises by less than 10 per cent, then we say that the firm has experienced decreasing returns to scale.

If a firm is experiencing economies of scale then the LRAC will be falling, whereas diseconomies of scale will lead to rising LRAC. If a 10% rise in inputs leads to a 10% rise in output then a firm is experiencing constant returns to scale and the LRAC will be constant. Increasing returns to scale are thus a source of economies of scale.

Figure 4.7: Returns to scale

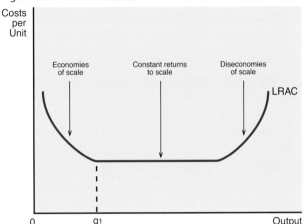

The output level of 0q1 in Figure 4.7 represents the **minimum efficient scale (MES)**, which produces the lowest average cost of production in the long run. The points of MES vary considerably between firms and this explains why some industries comprise many small firms while others include a few large firms. MES is the level of output beyond which average costs fall no further. The MES shows the lowest level of output that a firm can produce and still be cost competitive. The shape of the long term average cost curve will vary from industry to industry, and also change over time due to technological factors.

Sources of internal economies of scale

Technical economies
These result in increases in productivity, arising from the process of production when the scale of a firm's operations increases. There are three key technical economies of scale.

(i) **Specialisation:** The bigger the firm the greater the opportunities for increased specialisation. Specialist machinery will allow the firm to increase capital and labour productivity (total factor productivity) thus lowering long run average costs.

(ii) **Indivisibilities:** A firm will always be able to increase its productivity by using more efficient capital. For example, if two machines perform exactly the same task, but one machine produces three times as much per hour than the other productivity will be increased by using it. However, capital equipment with high levels of productivity is often large and expensive needing a high throughput. In many cases it is indivisible in the sense that it is not available in a smaller version. Assembly lines for mass-produced cars, nuclear power stations and oil refineries are examples of large pieces of capital equipment which cannot be scaled down below a certain level of production. Only when a firm's output grows will it be able to afford to use these large pieces of capital equipment; at low levels of output these indivisible units of capital equipment would be under-utilised and the firm would be operating with excess capacity.

(iii) **Linkage of processes (multiples):** Products often need a number of separate processes to produce a finished item. If the first machine in a production process has a capacity of 20 units per hour and the second machine has a capacity of 15 units per hour the firm will require an output of a least 60 units per hour to use all its machinery to its full capacity and maximise productivity (3 of the first machine and 4 of the second) This assumes only a two stage production process. Thus the larger the level of

output the more efficient is the linkage of processes because a firm with an output of 40 units would have capacity under-utilised in the second stage of production.

(iv) **Economies of increased dimensions:** The law of increased dimensions applies mainly to industries involved in distribution and transportation. It means that doubling the height and width of, for example a storage warehouse, leads to a more than proportionate increase in the storage capacity of the building. The same principle applies to container vessels and oil tankers. This means that storage and transportation costs per unit will fall as size increases. The common sight of very large container ships at sea is evidence of this. The largest container ship in the world is currently the MSC Oscar which is shorter in length than the previous record holder the CSCL Globe but it can carry 124 more containers. It is 396m (1,300ft) long and has a capacity of 19,224 standard containers.

Marketing economies

Large firms gain from the benefits of bulk purchase because they are powerful enough to buy raw materials and other inputs at a discount. They can often demand huge discounts from their suppliers by threatening to take their business elsewhere using their huge buying power as a threat. This has often been alleged of supermarkets in the UK who have been accused of demanding such large discounts from suppliers such as farmers and meat processors that the latter are unable to make even minimal levels of profit. This has been particularly true of dairy farmers.

Firms, which are large, can use their own lorry fleets and bulk containers to transport goods to markets. The scale of the method of transport used means that cost per unit transported falls for firms using bulk transportation methods such as supertankers for oil. In addition large firms are able to buy advertising time on TV and radio with discounts from broadcasters. The same principle can apply to the purchase of advertising space in newspapers and magazines.

Financial economies

Large firms are often able to obtain finance more cheaply and easily than smaller firms as they have a higher credit rating. Banks may consider them to be a lower risk than smaller firms partly because of a more established reputation and also because they can offer more collateral security. Accordingly large firms can often obtain more favourable repayment terms and lower rates of interest than smaller firms; hence lowering costs per unit.

Managerial economies

Once a firm becomes larger it can employ specialist managers and departments to deal with key functional areas such as marketing, finance, sales and purchasing. The expertise of specialist personnel can help to make the organisation run more efficiently at a higher level of productivity and hence a lower unit cost.

Research economies of scale

Large firms have the resources to commit themselves to major research programmes in search of new products. To be a successful global car producer firms need to be large. MG Rover failed in part because it was not large enough to command the research resources to develop new cars to replace its ageing models. It could not compete globally with the likes of Toyota, Nissan and Ford. It was said that MG Rover was "too small to be big and too large to be small". This meant that it was too small to develop, produce and sell new cars for the global car market but too large to be a niche producer such as Morgan, TVR and Bristol Cars. Similarly large pharmaceutical firms such as GSK, Astra Zeneca and Pfister have the resources to take research risks with many ideas in the development of major new drugs in medical science some of which may never reach the market. The latter point is often called **risk-bearing economies of scale**.

Diseconomies of scale

It is possible that beyond a certain level of output further increases in the scale of production might lead to diseconomies of scale. The suggestion is that large firms can eventually become more difficult to manage. This can be because of problems organising and coordinating the firm's activities resulting in slow and ineffective decision-making and poor communication. There is thus an ineffective flow of information between parts of the company. In very large firms the motivation of workers suffers as they feel a 'disconnect' between them and the management. As a result productivity falls leading to a rise in costs. Diseconomies of scale chiefly result from the managerial side of the business and can result in the firm splitting itself into separate operating divisions or even demerging.

External economies of scale

The above analysis of economies of scale only deals with **internal economies of scale**, so called because they arise from within the firm itself. There are also external economies of scale which arise from changes within the whole industry and which benefit all firms within that industry, whatever their size. A technological breakthrough may reduce the costs per unit of all the firms in an industry, shifting the long run average cost curve downwards at all levels of output (see Figure 4.8).

Figure 4.8

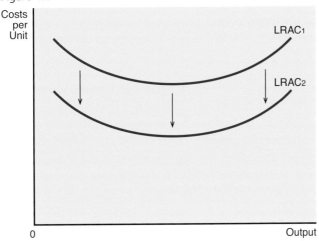

Another important external economy relates to the concentration of an industry in a particular geographical area. In the UK car manufacture was traditionally concentrated in the Midlands, textiles in Lancashire and shipbuilding in the North-East. There are now new examples of what is called **external economies of concentration**. 'Silicon Fen' is the name given to the region around Cambridge, which is home to a large cluster of high technology knowledge based businesses which focus on software, electronics and biotechnology. This growth has obviously been developed thanks to links with the university, and there have been suggestions that an improved rail link between Oxford and Cambridge would expand this further creating a 'brain belt' between the two old university towns.

Similarly there has been the growth of a cluster of high tech firms linked to Formula 1 racing in the motor sport industry in Northamptonshire and Oxfordshire. The use of Silverstone in Northamptonshire for the British Grand Prix has obviously been a factor in the growth of this industry in the UK. According to the Motorsport Industry Association; "The companies found within this motorsport cluster provide engineering solutions and act as a global centre for the production of performance cars. A supporting services industry offering specialised legal, financial and insurance services has also built up around these world-class design and manufacturing businesses." When a number of firms making the same product locate close together the local labour force is geared up to the skill requirements of the industry. Local colleges often run courses geared to employment in the industry and specialist support firms are attracted to the area to provide parts or specialist services. Local government may improve transport links in the area. When a whole area is geared to the needs of one industry which commands a lot of the employment, the benefits of lower costs feed through to all firms. The strength of the Lancashire textile industry in the early part of the last century owed much to external economies of scale, as does the City of London with banking and financial services.

A cluster of high tech firms linked to Formula 1 racing has grown up near Silverstone, home of the British Grand Prix.

External diseconomies of scale are the disadvantages that arise due to high levels of production as a result of an increase in the number of firms in an industry – particularly if these firms concentrate in the same geographical area. It is possible that if too many firms from the same industry locate in one area local labour becomes scarce and firms have to offer higher wages to attract new workers, often poaching them from rival firms. Land and factory space can become scarce and rents begin to rise. Local roads become congested and so transport costs begin to rise. These problems are called **external diseconomies of scale** which will shift the long run average cost curve upwards. Most seriously if the whole industry goes into decline as a result of falling demand for its products then the whole region in which it is located will suffer very high **structural unemployment**. This happened with Lancashire textiles and the shipyards on the Tyne and the Clyde when cheaper imports made it impossible for UK firms to compete.

Economies of scope

When a firm increases the number of different goods it produces, long run average costs of production can fall. Economies of scope refer to efficiencies associated with the range of products available from a firm. Take, for example, a firm such as Procter and Gamble which produces a huge range of products not directly related to one another, from razors to toothpaste. They can afford to hire expensive graphic designers and marketing experts, who can use their skills across many different product lines. As the firm's management structure, design, marketing, administrative systems and distribution costs are spread over such a large product range this lowers the average cost of production for each product.

Revenue

Revenue for a firm is calculated by multiplying price by quantity demanded.

∴ **Total Revenue** = Price x Quantity

In Figure 4.9 Op_1 x Oq_1 = Total Revenue. This is the shown as the coloured rectangle.

If Total Revenue (TR) is divided by quantity (Q) then the result is Average Revenue (AR)

$$\therefore AR = \frac{TR}{Q}$$

Figure 4.9: Total and average revenue

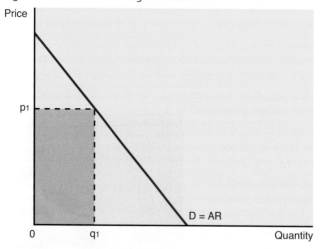

Also: $AR = \dfrac{TR}{Q} = \dfrac{P \times Q}{Q} = P$

Thus **Average Revenue** (AR) also equals price, which means that the demand curve is also the average revenue curve, sometimes called the price line.

Marginal Revenue (MR) is the addition to Total Revenue as a result of selling one more unit, which once calculated, can be shown on a diagram.

Price (£)	Quantity Demanded	TR	AR	MR	
10	1	£10	£10		
9	2	£18	£9	£8	= £18 - £10
8	3	£24	£8	£6	= £24 - £18
7	4	£28	£7	£4	= £28 - £24
6	5	£30	£6	£2	= £30 - £28
5	6	£30	£5	£0	= £30 - £30
4	7	£28	£4	£-2	= £28 - £30
3	8	£24	£3	£-4	= £24 - £28
2	9	£18	£2	£-6	= £18 - £24
1	10	£10	£1	£-8	= £10 - £18
0	11	£0	£0	£-10	= £0 - £10

The Marginal Revenue (MR) line shown in Figure 4.10 is at first positive and then negative. Where MR = 0 the firm will maximise its sales revenue. Each time average revenue falls by £1 marginal revenue falls by £2 and thus the gradient of MR is twice as steep as AR.

It is important to remember that the price elasticity of demand varies along the length of the demand curve. Over the full price range demand is perfectly elastic at the price axis and perfectly inelastic at the quantity axis. At points on the demand curve above X demand is progressively more price elastic whereas below point X demand is progressively more price inelastic. The point marked X is at the mid-point on the demand curve and also indicates unit elastic demand (price elasticity of demand = (-)1). If price is above p1 then a fall in price will raise sales revenue because MR is positive (demand is price elastic). If price falls to below p1 sales revenue will fall because MR is negative (demand is price inelastic). When MR = 0 at point X then total revenue is maximised as shown in the diagram.

Figure 4.10: Marginal, average and total revenue

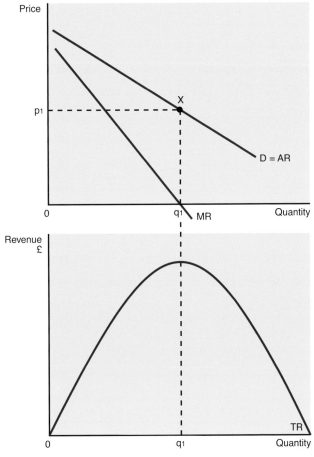

It is important to remember that when there is a change in demand not only does average revenue (AR) shift but also marginal revenue (MR). This is shown below in Figure 4.11 which illustrates a rise in demand. When drawing this diagram the gradient of MR should be twice as steep as that of AR. Marginal Revenue is always lower than the price (AR) that the firm is able to charge for the product being sold because each reduction in price causes the revenue from all units sold to decline. The marginal revenue (the increase in total revenue) is the price the firm gets on the additional unit sold, less the revenue lost by reducing the price on all other units that were sold prior to the decrease in the price.

Figure 4.11

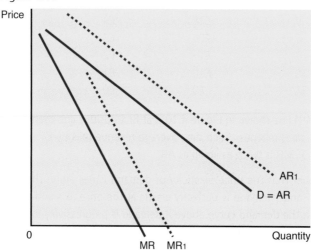

Question 4.1

You are given the following information:

Cost per tonne of fertiliser = £140; Fixed cost of land = £3000; (Assume that no further costs are incurred.)
Selling price of wheat = £2 per unit.

Tonnes of fertiliser applied to a fixed area of land	Total production (units)
0	1000
1	1100
2	1250
3	1500
4	1900
5	2150
6	2275
7	2350
8	2380
9	2330

(a) With reference to the above data, comment on the relationship between the application of fertiliser and the production of wheat.
(b) What level of fertiliser would a profit maximising farmer choose to apply? Show the amount of wheat produced and the profit earned. Justify your answer.

Source: ULEAC, Economics Paper 3, June 1983

Question 4.2

Given below are the cost and price data for a profit maximising firm.

Output Level per Period	Total Variable Costs (£)	Total Fixed Costs (£)
1	5	5
2	9	5
3	12	5
4	16	5
5	22	5
6	31	5
7	34	5
8	52	5
9	76	5
10	107	5

(a) Assume that the market price is constant at £18 per unit. At what level of output would profits be maximised?

(b) If the market price were to decline from £18, at what prices would the firm cease production (i) in the long run and (ii) immediately? (See Unit 7.)

Source: ULEAC, Economics Paper 3, June 1981

Question 4.3

Using the concept of price elasticity of demand to explain why price P_1 in Figure 4.10 will maximise sales revenue for the firm.

Question 4.4

Using the diagram below, explain what is meant by internal economies and internal diseconomies of scale.

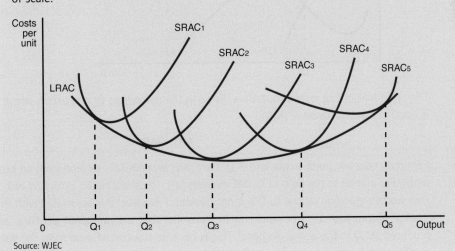

Source: WJEC

Unit 5: **The behaviour of the profit maximising firm**

Short run profit maximisation

Neo-classical economic theory assumes that firms aim to maximise profit, which is defined as the difference between revenue and cost. The point should be reinforced that by 'cost' economists mean the opportunity cost of the factors of production and that economic cost thus includes an allowance for normal profit (the level of profit which is just sufficient to keep the factors of production in their present use). The difference between revenue and cost is thus **supernormal/abnormal profit**.

Marginal analysis is commonly used to determine the profit maximising level of output for a firm. Figure 5.1 shows a firm facing a downward sloping demand curve, left to right. This tells us the price at which the firm will be able to sell a given number of units during a given period of time. The demand curve is the firm's average revenue curve too, because the price of the product is the revenue that will be gained from each unit of it sold. If the firm wishes to sell more of its product, it must reduce the price on *all* units of the good sold. The extra (marginal) revenue from the sale of one more unit is thus less than the average revenue (price). From a mathematical point of view the marginal revenue curve (MR) is twice as steep as the average revenue curve (AR).

Figure 5.1: Profit maximisation

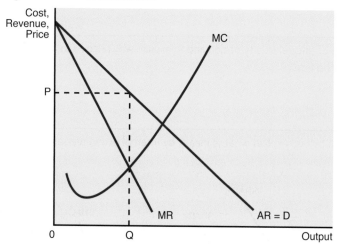

The profit maximising level of output is shown in the diagram as Q, and occurs where marginal cost (MC) is equal to marginal revenue (MR):

$$MC = MR$$

For proof, take any point to the left of Q. Here, MR exceeds MC, so producing an extra unit must add to profit. For a point to the right of Q, MC exceeds MR, so producing an extra unit will decrease profit. It is thus worth expanding output to Q but not beyond. Price level P is associated with the profit maximising level of output level Q. It is important to remember that the **marginal profit** is zero on the last unit produced (at Q in the above diagram). This is because the cost of producing the last unit (the marginal cost) is equal to the revenue from selling it (the marginal revenue).

Long run profit maximisation

The neo-classical assumption takes a short term view of profit maximising, in as much as it implies that a firm will adjust its price and output rapidly in response to changes in market conditions. However, if consumers dislike price changes, it may be the case that long run profit levels will be enhanced by the maintenance of a stable price. Thus it is possible that price will only be changed when it becomes clear that

Increased competition from new entrants often forces firms to cut margins or reduce costs.

a change in market conditions will persist into the long run. This is particularly so where a firm pursues a mark-up pricing policy (price = cost of production plus a percentage mark-up known as **cost-plus pricing**). The cost-plus approach to pricing involves calculating all the costs associated with producing and marketing a product on a per unit basis and then adding a margin to provide a profit. The profit per unit can be shown as a percentage of the cost, when it is referred to as the **mark-up** or or as a percentage of the selling price, when it is called the **mark-on**, or margin.

$$\text{Mark-up} = \frac{\text{Selling Price} - \text{Cost Price}}{\text{Cost Price}} \times \frac{100}{1}$$

$$\text{Mark-on} = \frac{\text{Selling Price} - \text{Cost Price}}{\text{Selling Price}} \times \frac{100}{1}$$

The only thing that will change the price charged is then a long run shift in cost conditions or possibly a change in market conditions. A severe recession or increased competition from new entrants often forces firms to cut their margins or find ways to reduce their costs. Long term profit maximising might entail forward-looking policies that would be rejected by a company more interested in short term profit levels. Unit 17 examines the issues associated with 'short termism'.

Question 5.1

If the price a profit-maximising firm can sell its output is fixed by the government it will produce at a level of output where

(a) average cost is equal to average revenue.

(b) average cost is minimised.

(c) marginal cost is equal to price.

(d) total revenue is maximised.

(e) total cost is minimised.

Unit 6: **Alternative goals for the firm**

The question as to the objectives that a firm will set itself is a complex one, and the standard neo-classical profit maximising assumption is regarded by many as too simplistic however important profit might be to a firm (see Unit 1).

Managerial theories of the firm

When a firm introduces revenue maximisation, sales maximisation or growth in market share as objectives this often illustrates the divorce between ownership and control in large organisations. Managerial theories are based on the assumption that managers control the company. Managers may have their own agenda, and wish to pursue goals such as maximising their own prestige or even simply enjoying an easy life. Sometimes perks and status are not tied directly to profit maximisation and thus managers make enough profit to prevent a shareholder revolt, while still enjoying the perks afforded by not striving to maximise profits.

Revenue maximisation

Figure 6.1 highlights the fact that a sales revenue maximising firm will expand output until MR is zero. This is because while MR is positive and demand price elastic, each extra unit sold adds to revenue. Selling extra units beyond the point where MR is zero would, on the other hand, reduce revenue because demand is price inelastic. The firm's output is thus Qsr and the price charged Psr, which contrasts with neo-classical profit maximising output of Qpm and price Ppm. If a firm pursues sales revenue maximisation it's likely to have a bigger share of the market than if it profit-maximised.

Figure 6.1: Sales revenue maximisation

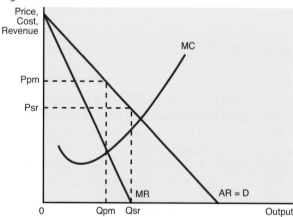

Ppm = Price to maximise profit
Psr = Price to maximise sales revenue

Sales maximisation

A firm might wish to maximise the number of units sold, in turn maximising its share of the market, although this goal would have to be pursued subject to a profit constraint. The firm could expect to sell a large number of units if it dropped its price far enough, but at some point cutting price any further will involve making a loss. Figure 6.2 shows the output and price of a firm, which wishes to maximise sales subject to the constraint of making at least normal profit. Output is thus set at the level where AR = AC because if price fell below Ps with output above Qs then AR<AC and losses would be made.

Figure 6.2: Sales volume maximisation subject to constraint of normal profit

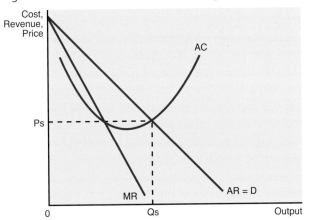

The divorce of ownership and control

Other theories result from debate about who is in control of the firm. Shareholders own the firm and are likely to want it to maximise profits for their dividends, but they have little direct input as to how the company should be run on a day-to-day basis. This is in the hands of a board of directors who may have other objectives in addition to making profits. Thus ownership of the company is divorced from control. This illustrates the **principal-agent problem** where the manager (the agent) does not always act in the best interests of the shareholders (the principal). It is important to establish where control of the company lies because the behaviour of the firm will largely be determined by this factor. It is worth noting that in recent years there has been an increase in the popularity of private limited companies whose affairs are not open to the same scrutiny as is the case with public limited companies (PLCs). Virgin Group and Arcadia, which includes Wallis, Top Shop and Dorothy Perkins, are private companies. Decision-making on key strategic objectives by the board of directors of a PLC is likely to be subject to more constraints than in a private limited company. A PLC's shares can be traded openly on the Stock Exchange and shares can thus be bought by anyone who then has rights to attend the Annual General Meeting and question board members. In recent years pressure groups such as Greenpeace have bought shares in PLCs who may have not, in their view, been taking enough care with environmental issues. These pressure groups may not be able to exert real power but they can articulate their viewpoints effectively. When Shell hosted its annual meeting of shareholders in The Hague, Netherlands in 2015 environment campaigners such as Greenpeace and Global Witness were there to challenge Shell's plans to drill for oil in the melting Arctic Ocean. In addition individual shareholders have used the AGM of PLCs to complain about directors' bonuses.

Behavioural theories

American economist Herbert Simon argued that decision-making within a company is the result of interaction between many competing groups within the firm. The rank and file workers might have different goals to those of the sales manager, for example, and the objectives of the sales manager are likely to be different to those of the production manager, and so on. The behaviour of the firm will then depend upon the balance of power between these competing groups. Reconciling the various competing groups within large organisations with many levels of management involves a decision making process from which emerges **'satisficing'**. Bargaining among managers will produce compromises which can be seen as satisfactory –

hence the term satisficing. Minimum targets may be set for a range of objectives such as market share or sales turnover. This can carry on until more difficult trading conditions occur, then managers will remove organisational slack (**X-inefficiency**) in the firm by possibly reforming work practices and announcing redundancies for example.

Other goals

The special nature of an organisation might dictate its goals. Consider, for instance, the values that inspire worker-cooperatives or a company that is set up for charitable purposes. Many firms are now aware that they need to satisfy, as far as is possible, all the **stakeholders** of the firm, i.e. customers, employees, shareholders, lenders etc. Stakeholders are people who have an interest in the activities of a firm. In particular industries objectives unique to that sector are obviously important. In the airline sector a key objective is the 'load factor' on each flight i.e. the percentage of seats filled. Airlines may be aiming for an 85% load factor for example. Load factors are important in businesses such as air travel where most of the costs are fixed. State-owned Network Rail probably places more emphasis on safety and maintenance than its more profit-motivated predecessor, Railtrack. In addition ethical and environmental objectives have become more important to firms operating in sensitive areas of production such as oil and chemicals. It is common for large firms to produce an annual social audit of their activities which examines the positive and negative effects of the firm's operations on the wider society.

In the autumn of 2015 it was discovered that the car maker VW had installed a device in its diesel cars that caused the emissions from the exhaust to perform better when the car was under test in controlled conditions than when under normal driving conditions. Vehicles were fitted with a so called 'defeat device' to achieve these bogus results and VW admitted that 11 million of its vehicles had this device in their engines, 1.2 million of them in the UK. This policy allowed the firm to sell more of their powerful luxury cars because the bogus lower level of emissions recorded in test conditions meant lower road tax for the owners. Although this practice leads to higher profits in the short term this unethical and illegal practice has potentially huge negative effects on brand image if it is discovered. Large businesses such as VW produce reports on Corporate Social Responsibility (CSR) and have sustainability goals but as Matthew Lynn of *The Daily Telegraph* said in September 2015; "What this surely tells us is that CSR has become a racket – and a dangerous one. It allows companies to parade their virtue, and look good, while internal standards are allowed to slip."

Question 6.1

Many firms aspire to broader objectives than merely profit maximisation as seen below with BP.

BP Group Values

What we do

We deliver energy to the world.

We find, develop and produce essential sources of energy. We turn these sources into products that people need everywhere.

The world needs energy and this need is growing. This energy will be in many forms. It is, and will always be, vital for people and progress everywhere.

We expect to be held to high standards in what we do. We strive to be a safety leader in our industry, a world-class operator, a good corporate citizen and a great employer. We are BP.

What we stand for

We care deeply about how we deliver energy to the world.

Above everything, that starts with safety and excellence in our operations. This is fundamental to our success.

Our approach is built on respect, being consistent and having the courage to do the right thing. We believe success comes from the energy of our people. We have a determination to learn and to do things better. We depend upon developing and deploying the best technology, and building long-lasting relationships.

We are committed to making a real difference in providing the energy the world needs today, and in the changing world of tomorrow. We work as one team. We are BP.

Safety

Safety is good business. Everything we do relies upon the safety of our workforce and the communities around us. We care about the safe management of the environment. We are committed to safely delivering energy to the world.

Respect

We respect the world in which we operate. It begins with compliance with laws and regulations. We hold ourselves to the highest ethical standards and behave in ways that earn the trust of others.

We depend on the relationships we have and respect each other and those we work with. We value diversity of people and thought. We care about the consequences of our decisions, large and small, on those around us.

Excellence

We are in a hazardous business and are committed to excellence through the systematic and disciplined management of our operations. We follow and uphold the rules and standards we set for our company. We commit to quality outcomes, have a thirst to learn and to improve. If something is not right, we correct it.

Courage

What we do is rarely easy. Achieving the best outcomes often requires the courage to face difficulty, to speak up and stand by what we believe. We always strive to do the right thing. We explore new ways of thinking and are unafraid to ask for help. We are honest with ourselves and actively seek feedback from others. We aim for an enduring legacy, despite the short-term priorities of our world.

One Team

Whatever the strength of the individual, we will accomplish more together. We put the team ahead of our personal success and commit to building its capability. We trust each other to deliver on our respective obligations.

Source: British Petroleum

Question: To what extent do the values set out above conflict with profit maximisation?

Question 6.2

	Price (£)	Number Sold
A publisher has to decide the price at which to sell a new book. He estimates that the costs incurred before publication amount to £10,000 and that variable costs amount to £1 a copy. In addition, he has agreed to pay the author royalties at a rate of 10 per cent of sales revenue. The publisher's best estimate of the number of books he would sell at different prices is as shown:	1.00	60,000
	1.25	40,000
	1.50	35,000
	1.75	20,000
	2.00	10,000

(a) Which of the above prices would maximise the publisher's profits?

(b) Which of the above prices would maximise the author's royalties?

Source: ULEAC, Economics p.3, June 1977

The above model has had great significance over the last sixty years when examining markets. The structure-conduct-performance analysis can be shown in a diagram as set out below.

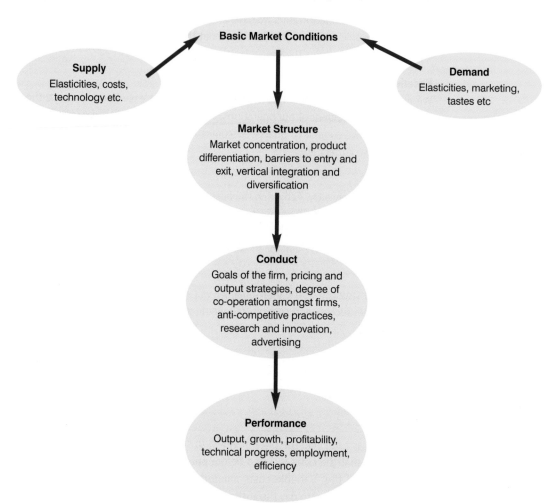

Basic market conditions (demand and supply) determine the structure of a market (either competitive or monopolistic), which in turn will determine conduct (such as pricing) and performance (such as profitability). The implication is that markets, which are highly concentrated such as monopolies, are able to set high prices or engage in anti-competitive practices, which result in abnormal profits and efficiency losses. The structure-conduct-performance can give competition authorities a valuable reference point for firms and industries, which may be acting anti-competitively.

In recent years the structure-conduct-performance model has been criticised, specifically by the contestable market approach developed by William Baumol. His view was that it did not matter whether an industry was highly concentrated (dominated by a few firms) as long as firms were free to enter and leave the market without making losses. A **contestable market** is one where there are low entry and exit barriers and low sunk costs. A **sunk cost** is one which cannot be recovered when a firm leaves an industry such as advertising and research expenditure. This view suggests that government intervention to control monopolies and mergers should be based on a policy, which examines the contestability of the market as well as its structure. This and other issues raised here are developed in the forthcoming units.

Unit 7: **Perfect competition**

Market characteristics:

1. Many buyers and many sellers.

2. All firms and consumers enjoy perfect knowledge of market conditions.

3. Homogeneous (identical) products.

4. Complete freedom of entry to, and exit from, the market in the long run (there are no barriers to entry; since cost advantages constitute a barrier to entry, this implies that all firms have identical cost structures). Such a market is thus perfectly contestable.

Conditions 1-3 combine to render each firm a **price taker**: Small in relation to the market and producing a product identical to that of many other firms, the firm has to accept the market price. Any attempt to raise prices will lead to complete substitution away from the firm's product, given the perfect knowledge enjoyed by consumers. As a price taker, the firm can sell as much as it wishes at the going market price, that is to say it is faced by a perfectly elastic demand curve. This results in a constant average revenue (AR) and marginal revenue (MR), but how much the firm will sell is subject to the constraints of its cost curves. The perfect knowledge of firms in this type of market means that there is no incentive for technological change as any idea or process introduced by one firm would immediately be available to all the others. Thus there would be no way for a firm to recover its research costs.

Short run equilibrium

Figure 7.1 shows the industry equilibrium on the left hand side. The right hand side illustrates the situation facing each individual firm operating in the market. They accept the price determined at industry level and then supply the quantity of output that will maximise the firm's profits. In the short run, it is possible that market conditions will permit individual firms to make supernormal profits, as represented by the shaded area in the diagram (the excess of AR over AC multiplied by output). It is important to note that the profit maximising level of output of the firm QF is not at minimum average cost in the short run.

Figure 7.1: Short run equilibrium under perfect competition

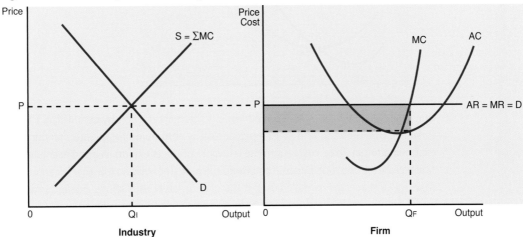

Long run equilibrium

Freedom of entry ensures that only normal profit will be made in the long run, as any short term supernormal profits will attract new firms into the market and erode profits. As new firms enter, the industry's supply curve shifts to the right (S→S1) lowering the market price (P→P1). Figure 7.2 depicts the long run

equilibrium position. Note that were losses to be experienced in the short run, the long run would see firms leaving the industry and the price rising to restore long run equilibrium. Firms will continue to enter or leave the industry until normal profits are made, at which point there is no further incentive to enter or leave the industry.

Figure 7.2: Long run equilibrium under perfect competition

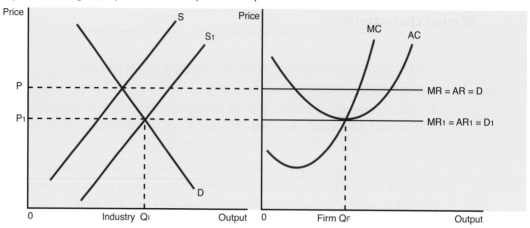

The firm's supply curve

The fact that MR is equal to price for the firm operating under conditions of perfect competition, combined with the MR = MC profit maximising condition, allows us to find the output level of the firm at any given price simply by reading across from that price to the MC curve. In other words, the firm's MC curve is its supply curve, as highlighted in Figure 7.3.

Figure 7.3: Construction of the firm's supply curve

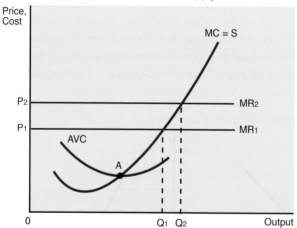

One point of qualification is required here. If the market price is not sufficient for the firm to cover its variable costs, then the firm faces a bigger loss by continuing to operate than by ceasing production and continuing to pay fixed costs (until the relevant contracts expire). A good example would be a steel works which ceases production because the world price of steel falls so low that it cannot cover even its variable costs (price < average variable cost). If the price of steel rises above average variable cost then the steel works can reopen in the short term because some contribution is being made towards fixed costs. These fixed costs such as rents, security, insurance etc would have to be paid even if the firm temporarily ceased production. Thus if price exceeds average variable cost then production is worthwhile, at least in the short term. The firm's supply curve is therefore the section of its MC curve rising above its average variable cost (AVC) curve, and point A on the diagram above is known as the '**shut down point**' in the **short run** where price equals average variable cost.

Average total cost includes normal profit measured in terms of the opportunity cost of resources. If a firm cannot make a normal profit it is making profits below a level that the same resources could earn in their next most profitable activity. A failure to make normal profits i.e. when price is below average cost, will mean that in the long run the firm will exit the industry. Thus a minimum requirement for a firm to stay in an industry in the **long run** is that price equals average cost (see Unit 1).

The industry's supply curve is derived by the horizontal summation of the supply curves of all the individual firms operating in the market.

Question 7.1

Consider the accompanying graph, and then answer the questions.

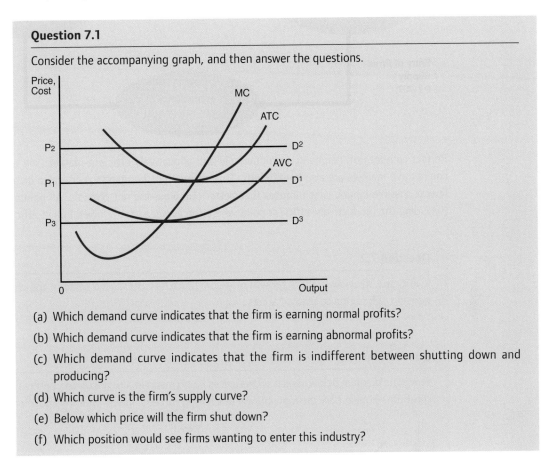

(a) Which demand curve indicates that the firm is earning normal profits?

(b) Which demand curve indicates that the firm is earning abnormal profits?

(c) Which demand curve indicates that the firm is indifferent between shutting down and producing?

(d) Which curve is the firm's supply curve?

(e) Below which price will the firm shut down?

(f) Which position would see firms wanting to enter this industry?

Do perfectly competitive markets exist?

The model explained in this unit is a theoretical abstract. That is to say that no real world industry possesses all of the characteristics of the perfectly competitive market structure.

The model remains a useful analytical tool, however, for by estimating how close a market is to being perfectly competitive, we can predict how closely the behaviour of the market will conform to the predictions of the model. Given that perfectly competitive markets produce desirable outcomes (see Unit 12) the model also presents an ideal at which to aim. This can be useful for industry regulators and the Competition and Markets Authority.

Some markets that approximate to perfect competition are those for agricultural produce, foreign currency exchange and buying and selling shares on the Stock Exchange. In the agricultural sector small-scale dairy farmers produce a homogeneous product (milk). There are many sellers and the farmers are price takers as they have no control over price individually. In recent years the plight of dairy farmers in the UK has resulted in many of them leaving the industry as a result of low prices for their milk. They were clearly unable to earn normal profit. In the foreign exchange market there are many dealers in currencies, which are homogeneous. Each €100 note looks the same to a buyer, and dealers in currency do not individually affect the exchange rate.

Summary

Perfect Competition

Short Run
Abnormal profit possible
AR > AC

Short Run
Losses possible
AC > AR

∴ **Entry of firms**
↑ Supply
↓ P (↓AR)

Long Run
Normal profits
AC = AR

Exit of firms
↓ Supply
↑ P (↑AR)

Perfect competition results in a productively and allocatively efficient market (see Unit 12). Perfectly competitive markets are also **X-efficient**. This means that the market produces a given output with the fewest possible inputs, which implies that better outcomes are not possible. All points on the cost curve (including the productively-efficient point where the average cost is lowest) are X-efficient.

Question 7.2

Investigate the view that the growth of e-commerce has introduced some of the characteristics of perfect competition to many markets.

Question 7.3

Study the diagram below, which shows losses being made in a perfectly competitive industry in the short run. Explain how the industry will reach long run equilibrium from this position.

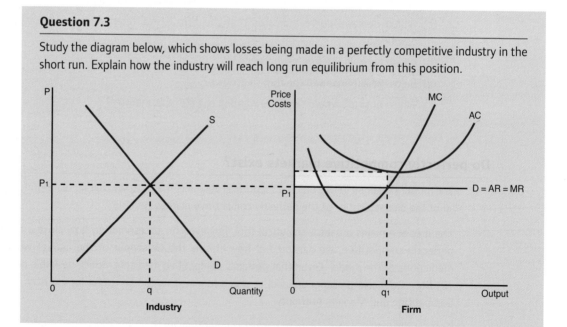

Industry

Firm

Question 7.4

Using the diagrams in this unit examine whether perfectly competitive firms are always productively efficient.

Unit 8: **Monopoly**

Of the market structures recognised by neo-classical theory, monopoly lies at the opposite end of the spectrum from perfect competition. By definition, a monopoly market is one in which only one seller operates. From a legal point of view, however, monopoly is taken to exist wherever one firm (or a cartel, a number of firms acting in collusion) enjoys a market share in excess of 25 per cent (see Unit 15). Such a definition is required because a market share of this magnitude may be sufficient to confer substantial control over prices. Good examples of monopolies in the UK are the water companies such as Thames Water who are a **pure monopoly** to domestic customers in geographical areas. Pure monopolies have a 100% market share. Durex has an 85% UK market share and a 30% global market share.

Market characteristics

1. Only one firm

2. High enough barriers to entry to prohibit new entry in both the short run and long run
These **barriers to entry** take one or more of a number of forms:

(a) **Capital costs and expertise.** e.g. firms find it hard to break into the oil business because large amounts of expertise are needed to compete with existing oil companies.

(b) **Economies of scale.** In some industries economies of scale are very large. This will act as a barrier to entry because any new firm entering the market is likely to be small in the first instance and therefore have higher average costs than existing producers. In natural monopolies (see Unit 12) economies of scale are so great that it is unprofitable for more than one firm to exist in an industry.

(c) **Legal restrictions.** Patents give legal protection to inventions by firms or individuals meaning that the owner of the patent has the right to stop anyone from making or using the invention without the owner's permission. This right is granted by the UK Intellectual Property Office and enforceable in a court of law. A patent can last for up to 20 years giving the holder of the patent time to recoup the financial outlay from its initial development. In other words, a patent is a right to stop competition for the invention for a limited period, effectively giving the patent holder monopoly power. In order to retain these rights, a patent holder must renew the patent regularly – first, on the fourth anniversary of the patent filing date, and then each subsequent year up to a maximum of 20 years.

However, this right to stop competition exists only in the country for which a patent has been granted. The holder of the patent may license it, allowing others to use the invention, paying the holder royalties. Alternatively, the patent holder can sell the patent to someone else who might be better able to exploit it commercially. Patents act as a significant barrier to entry in many industries. Pharmaceutical companies such as GlaxoSmithKline (GSK) rely heavily on the patents they hold. This enables them to gain returns on their enormous research costs without fear of copies appearing from competitors. Pharmaceutical companies are constantly challenged to stay one step ahead of expiring patents. Drugs have 20-year patents but once the patent has been registered there follows a lengthy period of development, clinical trials and then acceptance by the regulatory authorities in the country where sales will take place. This does not leave much time to reap the benefits of the monopoly protection from the patent. When drugs are on patent they are very costly for health authorities, but once the patent expires for a drug the patent holder's market share shrinks rapidly as other companies quickly offer cheaper generic alternatives. In recent years the US pharmaceutical Pfizer has struggled to find growth as sales continue to be hit by the loss of patent protection on highly profitable drugs. The company's loss of patent exclusivity on the world's former top-selling drug, cholesterol fighter Lipitor, has badly hit its drug revenues along with Celebrex which treats arthritis. Teva Pharmaceuticals and other top generic drug makers are looking to pounce on Pfizer's expiring patents. Pfizer has indicated

that it may either pursue a merger, or break itself up – a demerger – to solve this problem. In 2014 Pfizer tried to push through a £69bn acquisition of UK-based AstraZeneca, which would have given Pfizer a new set of cancer and Alzheimer's drugs with patent protection. In the end the persistent rejection of the offer by AstraZeneca's board of directors and intervention by senior UK politicians saw off Pfizer's attempt at a takeover. The huge cost of developing groundbreaking drugs (about $1.5bn) has led to mergers and acquisitions in the pharmaceutical industry in recent years as they seek the benefits of **research economies of scale**. In 1990 the market share of the top ten pharmaceutical companies totalled 28%; by 2014 it had risen to 44%. Some would argue that monopoly, like perfect competition, provides little incentive for research and innovation. However, monopolies often have sufficient profit to plough into research and the market power to reap the benefits from innovation, a view held by Schumpeter (dynamic efficiency), see Unit 12.

The UK's **Patent Box** regime for the taxation of intellectual property came into force in April 2013. Companies liable to UK tax can have the profits they earn from their patented inventions (and certain other innovations) taxed at a lower level of corporation tax, only 10%. The relief is to be phased in over 4 years leading to a tax rate of 10 per cent by April 2017. However the European Commission has indicated that the patent box constitutes unlawful state aid – and against EU regulations. Nonetheless the UK Government has confirmed its commitment to retaining a Patent Box scheme once reforms to it are agreed, but has announced it will close to new entrants by June 2016 and be abolished by June 2021.

For many years Royal Mail had a legal monopoly over the letterpost but this has been eroded in recent years partly by technological change and partly by the liberalisation of the postal sector. Until the late 1980s only the state owned National Coal Board was legally allowed to mine for coal in the UK.

(d) **Control of a scarce resource or input.** e.g. The De Beers Syndicate in South Africa enjoyed sole access to what was almost the only land on which diamonds could be mined, although the syndicate's dominance has recently been threatened by new sources in Russia and Africa. Ownership of the sole supply of raw materials gives a producer a powerful weapon against possible entrants. Backward vertical integration of this kind also applies in the UK electricity market where energy companies own power generation facilities.

(e) If an existing firm has better information about the way the industry works than the potential new entrant it will take expensive time for new entrants to acquire this know-how. Existing firms in a market have extensive knowledge of the supply chain and the customer base giving them a big advantage over potential entrants. This **information imbalance** is a reality in many markets and a significant barrier to entry. The technical name for this is **information asymmetry**.

(f) **Advertising.** If existing firms spend heavily on advertising, new firms will have to do so as well, if they are to compete on equal terms. Advertising drives up average costs, but does build up brand loyalty.

(g) **Brand proliferation.** If existing firms provide a wide range of similar products but with slightly different characteristics, it will be harder for any new firm to find a niche in the market. In this way a three-firm concentration ratio (the percentage of the market supplied by the largest three firms) of around 90% has been achieved by Kellogg's, Weetabix and Nestlé in the cereal industry. See also predatory and entry limit pricing (Unit 11).

When examining entry barriers it is often convenient to split them into structural and behavioural barriers. **Structural barriers** are not deliberately erected by existing firms and are therefore quite innocent. Start-up costs and those relating to economies of scale would fall into that category. **Behavioural barriers** are erected by the firms to deliberately prevent the entry of a new firm and these may include limit pricing and refusal to allow access to a scarce raw material supply. Some years ago there was controversy over British Telecom allowing other internet suppliers access to the 'local loop' was seen as a behavioural barrier to entry and investigated by the Competition Commission with a view to BT 'unbundling' it.

To ensure that rival telecom operators had equal and fair access to BT's local network Openreach was created in 2006 following an agreement between BT and the regulator Ofcom. Openreach manages BT's local network which connects customers to their local telephone exchange. Although Openreach is owned by the BT group of companies, it is operated independently of the BT company. Sky, TalkTalk and Vodafone who pay BT to access the network have all called for Openreach to be split completely from BT, saying the current setup is a "conflict of interest". The Openreach network is the most extensive of the fibre broadband networks in the UK and these companies all want better access to it, claiming a complete split from BT will increase incentives to invest and improve competition. Ofcom, the regulator, have stopped short of a complete split with BT and said that Openreach should be a wholly owned subsidiary of BT with an independent board for budget and strategy. BT's rivals are now allowed to lay their own fibre optic cables within the Openreach network.

Entry and Exit barriers lead to a misallocation of resources because factors of production cannot move freely.

3. Exit barriers

In some industries there are significant costs for a firm to pay when it decides to leave an industry. These closure costs arise as a result of redundancies to workers, landscaping the site, meeting environmental clear-up costs, disposal of equipment, etc. Firms facing huge exit costs may decide to carry on operating in activities they might otherwise leave because of huge closure costs. The US Steel industry was originally in this position in the late 1990's as cheap imports poured into the USA. President Bush's tariffs on imported steel kept production going in many plants. The US steel industry has firms which are unable to shut down inefficient plants. The price of closure is too high especially with redundancy costs, pension fund liabilities, health care liabilities, and environmental liabilities. Bethlehem Steel had a massive burden of legacy costs with 70,000 pensioners and 130,000 members of its healthcare plan. The long-term liability totalled almost $10bn. The costs of closure often thus exceed the cost of running the steel mills. After a decline in the US steel industry and management problems leading to the company's 2001 bankruptcy, Bethlehem Steel was dissolved and the remaining assets sold to International Steel Group (ISG) in 2003. In 2005, ISG merged with Mittal Steel, now known as ArcelorMittal (see Question 8.4).

Firms may stay in an industry as long as they can cover their variable costs and make a contribution to fixed costs (see Unit 7). In the short run firms carry on because of the huge costs of closure (exit costs) and become what is known as 'Zombie' firms.

Similar exit barriers resulting from high employee liabilities faced the troubled US car manufacturers, Ford, GM and Chrysler, in the recent recession. Exit barriers can act as an entry barrier because if firms know that it is difficult to leave an industry they may not try to enter it in the first place. Entry and exit barriers lead to a misallocation of resources because factors of production cannot move freely from one activity to another. It is important to remember that such costs act as both an exit and an entry barrier. Heavy expenditure on advertising, as it is non-recoverable on exit, acts as a significant exit barrier. Sunk costs are non-recoverable costs when a firm leaves an industry. These include start up costs such as marketing, research and development as well as exploration costs, which exist in both the oil and gas industry and mining.

Rather bizarrely governments can act directly to prevent the exit of a firm. In 2005 a French judge ordered the Swiss food giant Nestlé to re-open a loss making factory. Nestlé were told to re-launch production at the chocolate and Nescafé plant outside Marseilles which employed 427 workers. Nestlé called the ruling 'unbelievable and unprecedented' claiming that it abridged its basic freedom to manage its operations and that the loss-making plant would never become profitable. In the US the Chapter 11 bankruptcy law provides an opportunity for a firm to stay in an industry when its financial difficulties would suggest that it should leave. In late 2011 American Airlines' parent company AMR Corporation filed for Chapter 11 bankruptcy protection which refers to a section of the US Bankruptcy Code. It protects a company from its creditors, giving it time to reorganise its debts or sell parts of the business. Hence exit from the industry is delayed or even prevented. American Airlines' rivals Delta and United both filed under Chapter 11 post the 9/11 terrorist attacks but have since returned to profitability after having successfully restructured their labour contracts and cut costs.

Equilibrium

Given the market characteristics, the downward sloping market demand curve must also be the demand curve for the monopolist's product. Consequently, the monopolist has the power to be a **price-maker**: It can set the price. If it does this, it then sells whatever quantity consumers are willing to buy at that price. If the monopolist prefers instead to choose the quantity to sell, it must then accept the corresponding price. It is for this reason that the monopolist is said to be 'constrained by his demand curve'. The monopolist is assumed to be a profit maximiser which means using MC = MR to set output.

Any abnormal profits (the orange shaded area in Figure 8.1) that are made can persist into the long run, because of the high barriers to entry. Accordingly, the short and long run equilibria are identical, as shown below. It is important to note that the red shaded area represents total costs (average cost x output).

Figure 8.1: Price and output under monopoly

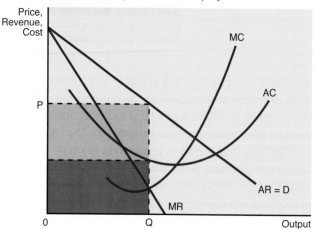

As the price charged by the monopolist is above its marginal cost it is said to be **allocatively inefficient**. In addition because output is below minimum average cost of production it is said to be **productively inefficient** (see Unit 12). Liëbenstein (1966) suggested that the allocative inefficiency of monopoly is likely to be less important than the internal inefficiency of '**X-inefficiency**'. As entry barriers protect a monopolist it is under little pressure to behave efficiently and minimise costs. Price can always be raised to maintain profits. Cutting costs involves unpopular and difficult decisions thus it is easier to keep this 'organisational slack' when a monopoly. How many firms with monopoly power have X-inefficiency? It could be argued that British Airways has had to tackle X-inefficiency after it lost its monopoly on certain routes and has had to face the competition from budget airlines. Some firms are often called **natural monopolies** which means that these firms minimise their long run average costs at a level of output which is close to the national level of demand. These monopolies are thus productively efficient and breaking them up to create competition simply results in several sub-optimal firms. Infrastructure businesses such as Network Rail (the rail system) and National Grid (electricity and gas) are seen as natural monopolies.

Figure 8.2

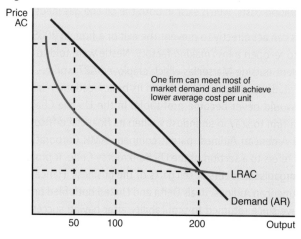

In the diagram above (Figure 8.2) it is more efficient to have one firm producing 200 units than four competing firms producing 50 units.

It can also be argued that monopoly can be a better outcome for a market than perfect competition as a result of the benefits of economies of scale enjoyed by a monopolist.

The diagram below (Figure 8.3) can be used to show the benefits of monopoly which arise from economies of scale. Assuming constant average costs the competitive firm has higher costs (LRACc) and its price is Pc. The monopolist operates with lower long run average and marginal costs (LRACm) and its price is Pm. Monopoly results in a higher price and a lower output which produces a welfare loss shown in red. However, there are significant cost savings resulting from the monopolist's economies of scale. These are shown as the green area and if this area is larger than the red area an industry is in theory better off being monopolised than competitive.

Figure 8.3

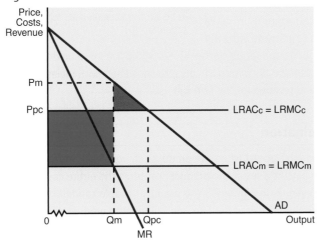

Price discrimination

Where market conditions permit, a monopolist might choose to price discriminate. This entails charging different prices to different groups of consumers for the same product or service. Firms with some degree of monopoly power have the ability to be price makers. If a single market price is charged, most purchasers of the product will enjoy consumer surplus. The term **consumer surplus** is used to represent the difference between the actual price paid by a consumer and the price they would have been willing to pay. For example, if I value a chocolate bar at 40p but purchase it for 25p, I enjoy 15p worth of consumer surplus. The area under the demand curve bounded by the vertical axis and the price line represents consumer surplus diagramatically. If the monopolist is able to raise the price above P (see Figure 8.4) to P1 for some customers, then it is able to appropriate some of their consumer surplus in the form of extra monopoly profits.

Figure 8.4: Consumer surplus and price discrimination

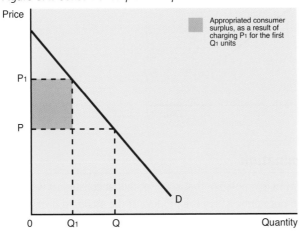

Perhaps the most important condition for price discrimination to be possible is that, after the market has been sub-divided, the sub-markets can be kept separate. Were it possible to buy the product in a low price sub-market and travel to a higher priced sub-market in order to re-sell at an intermediate price, price discrimination could not be effective. Time barriers, for example, keep markets for peak and off-peak travel separate; geographical barriers allow products to be sold for different prices in different countries. Markets can also be separated by age, charging less to pensioners and children than the standard price to adults. It is normal for each sub-market to have different price elasticities of demand with the

Time barriers keep markets for peak and off-peak travel separate.

highest prices being charged to the group of consumers with price inelastic demand and the lower prices to consumers with elastic demand. By raising the price to consumers with inelastic demand and lowering it to those with elastic demand revenue for the firm will rise.

First degree price discrimination

First degree price discrimination occurs when the producer charges each individual consumer the highest price they are prepared to pay. As a result the producer captures the entire consumer surplus, which then becomes extra producer revenue. In Figure 8.5 the producer is able to identify each potential consumer right up to the point where the price is so high no one will buy the product. It is difficult to find examples of this type of price discrimination although the Internet auction web site e-Bay has some similarities. A seller on e-Bay will capture the entire consumer surplus of the successful bidder if the auction is hotly contested. If for example a seller has five rare identical football programmes for sale on e-Bay and the auction is highly contested by say ten bidders then it is possible that the seller captures the entire consumer surplus of the five successful bidders. With this type of price discrimination the demand curve is actually the marginal revenue curve as in such an auction the price does not have to be lowered to sell additional units of the product.

Figure 8.5: First degree price discrimination

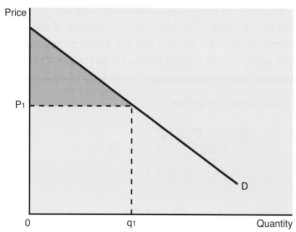

Second degree price discrimination

When a firm has surplus capacity it is possible that some potential consumers will be targeted by a lower price. These consumers would not normally buy the product at the standard price but a special lower price will attract them. This type of pricing is particularly popular when there is spare capacity and the low special price (marginal revenue) is higher than the marginal cost. Football stadiums in the lower divisions are often not filled to capacity and sometimes clubs introduce special offers for adults to bring children who only pay £1 to gain admission (often called 'kid a quid'). This kind of pricing adds to revenue but adds little to costs. As long as the special price is above marginal cost this type of pricing results in increased profits. In Figure 8.6 the shaded area represents the extra revenue from special lower prices.

Figure 8.6: Second degree price discrimination

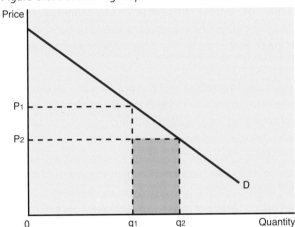

Third degree price discrimination

Figure 8.7 illustrates the process of maximising profit by distinguishing between two sub-markets. First, the monopolist determines his overall profit maximising output. The demand curve D_T is the total market demand curve, by implication the horizontal summation of the demand curves in the two sub-markets. Output (Q_T) is thus set at the level where the corresponding marginal revenue function (MR_T) is equal to marginal cost. The most profitable way to distribute this output between the two sub-markets is to do so in such a way that marginal revenue in the sub-markets is equated. To understand why, suppose marginal revenue were higher in sub-market A than sub-market B. By transferring a unit of output from sub-market B to sub-market A, more revenue would be gained than lost. Since the cost of production for one sub-market does not differ from production for the other, total cost remains unchanged and profits are increased. More units should be transferred until the marginal revenues are equal. Having decided on the appropriate output level for each sub-market, the price in each is determined by reading up to the relevant demand curve.

Figure 8.7: Third degree price discrimination

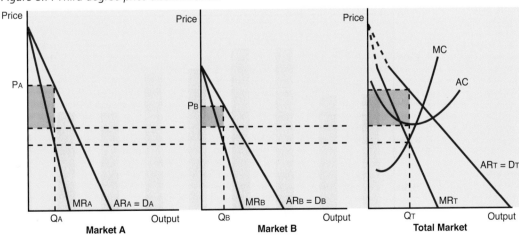

Note that if each sub-market had the same demand curve, the marginal revenue curves would be identical too, resulting in the same output and price level in each sub-market. Consequently, price discrimination can only be effective if the sub-markets have different demand curves. Price elasticity of demand must differ in each market. The firm will charge the higher price in the market where demand is less elastic, and thus less sensitive to price.

It is not necessary that price discrimination be limited to two sub-markets. The analysis above can be generalised to any number of sub-markets without affecting the conclusions. Indeed, if the firm could isolate each customer as a separate sub-market, it would charge each one just the price they were willing to pay, thereby appropriating the entire consumer surplus. This is known as perfect price discrimination or first degree price discrimination.

There are numerous examples of price discrimination from the real world. The most well known are associated with rail travel and telephone charges. Off-peak travel and phone calls from residential landlines are cheaper than at other times. This enables the producers to spread demand so that peak times are less congested. It does mean that peak time users with a more inelastic demand are possibly being over-charged.

Other examples include the main supermarkets charging more for some products in stores where their clientele is predominantly higher income and less in stores where shoppers are on lower incomes. British Airways has been accused of charging higher prices for a flight booked in the UK compared to someone booking the same flight overseas. Football fans have found that 'home' supporters are often charged less than 'away' fans to watch the same game. Have 'away' fans a more price inelastic demand as they are prepared to pay higher prices being a football club's most devoted supporters? The data below shows how the price charged on the M6 Toll varies according to vehicle type and the time of travel. It could be argued that only the price difference according to time of travel is an example of price discrimination. Heavy lorries impose much higher costs in road surface damage than cars and thus their toll should be higher.

M6 toll charges	Mon-Fri (06:00-23:00)		Sat-Sun (06:00-23:00)		Night (Mon-Fri) (23:00-06:00)	
Class	Non-Tag	Tag	Non-Tag	Tag	Non-Tag	Tag
Class 1 (e.g. motorbike)	£3.00	n/a	£2.80	n/a	£1.80	n/a
Class 2 (e.g. car)	£5.50	£5.22	£4.80	£4.56	£3.80	£3.61
Class 3 (e.g. car & trailer)	£10.00	£9.50	£8.60	£8.17	£6.60	£6.27
Class 4 (e.g. van or coach)	£11.00	£10.45	£9.60	£9.12	£8.60	£8.17
Class 5 (e.g. HGV or coach)	£11.00	£10.45	£9.60	£9.12	£8.60	£8.17

Source: M6 Toll (Midland Expressway Ltd)
Tag refers to a pre-payment system allowing regular users to pass through the toll without stopping to pay cash.

A typical easyJet return flight from Newcastle to Alicante shown below shows major price differences depending upon when the booking was made.

Figure 8.8: Price discrimination

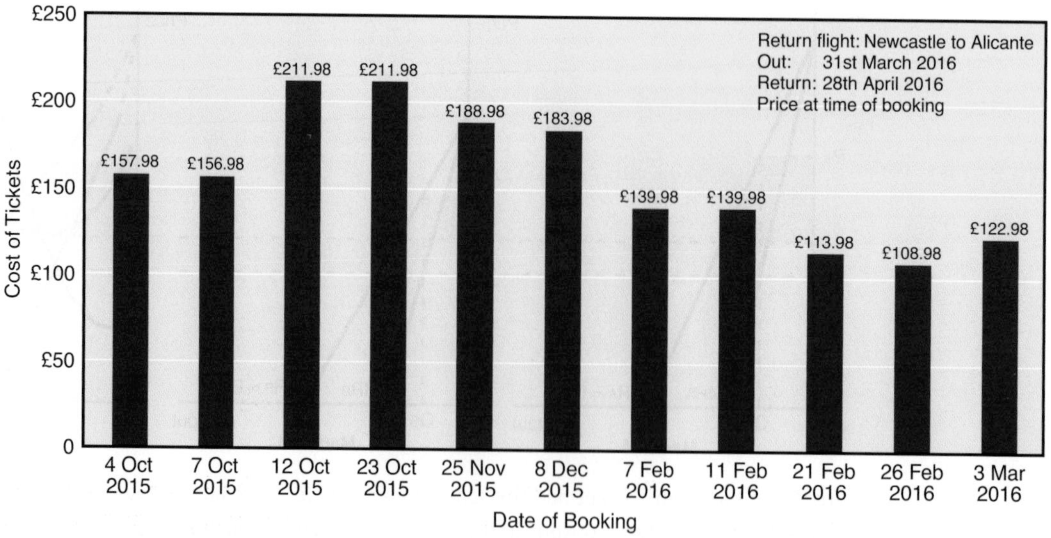

Airlines such as easyJet apply the principle of yield management when pricing their seats on flights, allowing them to maximise revenue from ticket sales. This means that most flights are close to full with a high load factor.

In recent years there have been numerous examples highlighted in the media where UK consumers have been charged more than consumers in other countries for the same product or service. Apple Music, Spotify and Napster have all been accused of charging more for their music streaming service in the UK compared to the European Union and the US. In 2015 the European Commission found that Disneyland Paris had been charging British holidaymakers up to 40% more than French tourists. This pricing policy is easy to implement when customers book online for tickets and accommodation. Similar practices have been found with British Airways flights and Eurostar tickets. The companies involved say that sales taxes and exchange rate conversions distort pricing and that prices are very similar to all nationalities when booked direct.

Many producers deny that some of the examples above are price discrimination and argue that price differences reflect cost differences, a different service or exchange rate differences. It is often argued that price discrimination not only benefits producers with higher profits, but consumers who would not normally have bought the product if there were a single price but may be tempted to buy at a special low off-peak price. Price discrimination also spreads demand away from peak-time use when travelling by train for example. Sometimes a firm will charge a higher price for its product in the home market where it faces little competition compared to the overseas market where the market is very competitive. There is no doubt that price discrimination by a profit maximising firm with some monopoly power will transfer some of the consumer surplus to the producer thus raising profit. Does price discrimination restrict, distort or prevent competition though? Certainly in some cases.

Is it worthwhile for a monopolist to advertise?

It would seem on the face of it that pure monopolists don't need to bother advertising as they have complete control of the market. However, advertising does help maintain the barriers to entry that exist against potential entrants, and it can be used to show that a monopolist is capable of being nice to consumers. In the past the water authorities in the UK, which are local monopolies, have often gone out of their way to inform their captive market that they are doing great things such as mending leaks and building new water treatment plants. In theory advertising will bring the monopolist even higher abnormal profits as the diagram below demonstrates. A successful advertising campaign will shift the demand curve and marginal revenue to the right and assuming the cost structure remains the same abnormal profits will rise shown by the shaded area in Figure 8.9. In reality advertising would increase fixed costs, increasing AC, thus reducing the rise in profits. Advertising would thus only be worthwhile if the increase in total revenue from sales is greater than the increase in total costs from advertising.

Figure 8.9: The increase in a monopolist's profit as a result of advertising

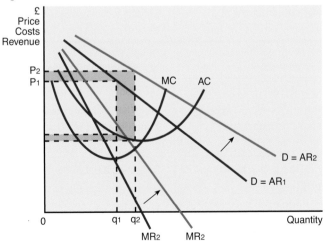

The diagram below (Figure 8.10) can be used to show the disadvantages of monopoly. The price in a competitive market would be Pc where price = marginal cost. However a monopoly would charge Pm and quantity would fall to Qm. The effect is to reduce the consumer surplus and increase the producer surplus which obviously benefits the monopoly. The deadweight loss indicates the market failure resulting from the monopolisation of a competitive industry.

Figure 8.10

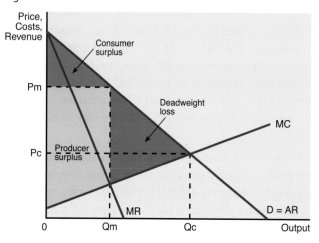

The benefits of monopoly	The drawbacks of monopoly
Abnormal profit provides funds for investment to maintain a competitive edge and also for R&D which are both important in global markets (dynamic efficiency).	Abnormal profit can mean little incentive to be efficient or to develop new products, leading to inefficiency.
There may be a need to match the large overseas competitors in a global market. Monopolies may also be a powerful counterbalance to a powerful buyer (monopsony).	High prices and lower output for consumers. Reduced consumer surplus compared to a competitive market.
Cross-subsidisation of markets may lead to an increased range of goods or services available to the consumer. It can thus supply goods that would otherwise not be provided.	Monopolies can waste resources by cross-subsidisation, using profits from one part of their organisation to finance losses in another, which is useful when predatory pricing and limit pricing (these are anti-competitive practices). (See Unit 10)
Price discrimination may raise total revenue which allows the survival of a product or service. Price discrimination can benefit some consumers who pay a lower price.	Monopolies may engage in price discrimination to raise producer surplus and reduce consumer surplus. This may involve charging higher prices to consumers with inelastic demand.
Monopolies can take advantage of economies of scale which lowers cost per unit. If this lowers prices the consumer surplus is higher than competition.	Monopolies are allocatively and productively inefficient. They are also more likely to carry X-inefficiency. (See Unit 12)
Marginal cost pricing as practised in perfect competition does not cover fixed costs in declining cost industries leading to huge losses.	By setting a price above marginal cost, prices are above the resource cost of producing the product.
Monopolies avoid the problems of duplication and wasteful advertising and some industries are possibly natural monopolies, e.g. local water companies, rail, gas and electricity infrastructures. (See Unit 12)	Monopolies deny consumers variety and choice which is available in competitive markets.

Source: Adapted from *Economics Made Simple*, G. Whitehead, with permission from Elsevier

Question 8.1

A monopolist has separated its customers into two markets, A and B. The prices and quantities in these two markets are as follows:

Market A			Market B	
Price (£)	Quantity		Price (£)	Quantity
10	10		5.00	10
9	20		4.50	20
8	30		4.00	30
7	40		3.50	40
6	50		3.00	50
5	60		2.50	60
4	70		2.00	70
3	80		1.50	80
2	90		1.00	90
1	100		0.50	100

(a) What conditions are necessary for the monopolist to be able to separate the two markets in this case? *(2 marks)*

(b) (i) On graph paper plot the monopolist's demand and marginal revenue curves in markets A and B. *(4 marks)*

(ii) Assuming that the marginal cost of production is constant at £1.90, what quantity will the monopolist sell in each market if it is a profit maximiser? *(2 marks)*

(iii) What price will the monopolist charge in each market? *(2 marks)*

(c) Comment on the relationship between the price elasticity of demand and marginal revenue in market B. *(4 marks)*

(d) Assume that the monopolist now cuts its price in market A by £0.50. What is the price elasticity of demand at the new price charged? *(3 marks)*

(e) Assume that the monopolist now faces an increase in the business rates payable on its premises. How will the profit maximising monopolist adjust the prices charged in each market? *(3 marks)*

Source: ULEAC, Economics Paper 2, January 1989

Question 8.2

An economist can measure the monopoly power of a firm by using the following equation:

$$\frac{\text{Price} - \text{Marginal Cost}}{\text{Price}}$$

The closer the answer is to 1 the greater the degree of monopoly power exercised by the firm, and the closer it is to 0 the more competitive the market. Explain the reasoning behind this.

Question 8.3

The Economist newspaper is sold in newsagents for £4.00 but a recent special scheme allowed secondary school pupils to buy 30 copies for just £2.

(a) With the aid of a diagram explain why this is an example of second-degree price discrimination.

(b) Using the terms marginal cost and marginal revenue explain why *The Economist* may still make a profit from the papers it sells to schools at such a discount.

Question 8.4

In the autumn of 2015 with global steel prices falling Thai company Sahaviriya Steel Industries (SSI) announced the closure of its steel making plant at Redcar on Teesside with a loss of 1,700 jobs. Steel, sold for £318 per tonne a year ago, was selling for only £191 and that meant that the plant was losing money. Exiting steel making is a complex decision because the assets are industry specific and often difficult and costly to dispose of. Once production ceases steel manufacture becomes very difficult and expensive to restart unless the plant is 'mothballed'. Many steel makers faced with low steel prices do 'mothball' their plant until prices rise and the plant can be re-opened. This was seen at Redcar which was mothballed in 2010 and re-opened in 2012 under new ownership. Since then about £1bn was invested at Redcar after the reopening of the blast furnace. However, 'mothballing' is an expensive process which involves keeping the coke ovens operational and would require over 300 staff at Redcar. Unfortunately SSI was put into liquidation by three Thai banks who are owed £430m by the company.

Compare the exit barriers in the steel industry to those in hairdressing.

The sun sets behind Teesside steelworks the day before the ovens were allowed to cool. Soon after, the steelworks were closed.

Unit 9: **Monopolistic competition**

Few markets conform closely to the models of either perfect competition or monopoly. Between these two extremes lie two forms of imperfect competition, namely monopolistic competition and oligopoly. Monopolistic competition as a market structure was first identified in the 1930s by Edward Chamberlin and Joan Robinson.

Market characteristics

Monopolistic competition shares many of the characteristics of perfect competition, except for the fact that products are non-homogeneous (i.e. there is **product differentiation**). Product differentiation occurs either through real differences in products or differences in image for otherwise identical products (possibly created or reinforced by advertising).

Differences in products' unique qualities create scope for **brand loyalty**: A consumer might be willing to pay a higher price for the product of one firm than for that of another in the same market. Each firm is a profit maximiser and makes its own decisions about price and output. Accordingly, the firm is not a price-taker, and each firm is faced by a downward sloping demand (AR) curve. Any firm raising its price will lose some business to its competitors, but brand loyalty will ensure that a firm will not suffer complete substitution away from its product. Because of the availability of substitutes the demand curve will be much more elastic than it would be for a monopolist operating in the same market. There are a large number of independent firms competing in the market. Good examples of monopolistic competition could include hairdressers, restaurants, taxi firms and fast food outlets. High street chemists are an interesting example of a market, which is a partial example of monopolistic competition with the majority of the market in the hands of independent outlets. Independent chemists have about a 40% share of the UK market. There are also bigger firms in the market such as Lloyds, Boots and Tesco. The major supermarkets have become increasingly involved in this sector, particularly since the ending of retail price maintenance on non-prescription drugs. Retail price maintenance meant that these products had to be sold at the same price in all retail outlets.

It is often confusing to students that a market structure with so little monopoly power for the firms is called monopolistic competition. The term 'monopolistic' refers to the small degree of monopoly power each firm possesses as a result of selling a branded product, which to some consumers will be unique.

They thus may see their local hairdresser, as the only place they would go to because they have been there for years and think the stylist is very good. The same can apply to restaurants. However, this monopoly power does not extend to all customers nor into the long run.

Short run equilibrium

The monopolistically competitive market conditions permit the possibility of short run supernormal profits (Figure 9.1) or losses.

Long run equilibrium

The lack of significant barriers to entry and exit ensures that normal profits are made in the long run. A situation of short run supernormal profit (as shown in Figure 9.1), for example, will induce new entry. As new firms enter the market the market share of existing firms is reduced, shifting the demand curve (AR) and marginal revenue (MR) inwards. This continues until AR is tangential to the average cost curve (AR = AC) at the profit maximising point. Given a situation of short run loss, some firms would leave the industry, also restoring long run equilibrium (see Figure 9.2).

Figure 9.1: Short run equilibrium under monopolistic competition

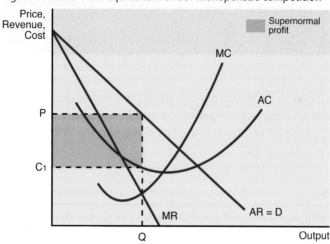

Figure 9.2 is a difficult one to draw. The following strategy is recommended:

1. Draw the average and marginal revenue curves.

2. Draw the average cost curve, with the point of tangency well above half way up the average revenue curve.

3. Label the price and quantity associated with this point of tangency (by virtue of the fact that the average revenue curve is also the demand curve).

4. Finally, draw the marginal cost curve. Ensure that it cuts the marginal revenue curve at the level of output depicted in step 3. It should also cut the average cost curve at that curve's lowest point.

Note that in both the short run and the long run price is above marginal cost and output is below minimum average costs. This means that monopolistic competition is an allocatively and productively inefficient market (see Unit 12).

Figure 9.2: Long run equilibrium under monopolistic competition

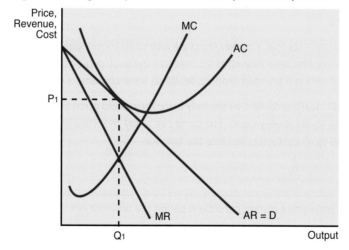

Question 9.1

Why might hairdressers, fast food outlets and Italian restaurants be examples of monopolistic competition?

How does monopolistic competition differ from perfect competition?

	Perfect Competition	Monopolistic Competition
Number of producers (sellers in the market)	Many	Many
Types of goods and services available for consumers		
Does the firm have control over their own prices?		
Is branding/marketing important?		
Are entry barriers zero, low or high?		
Does this market structure lead to allocative efficiency in the long run?		
Does this market structure lead to productive efficiency in the long run?		

Source: tutor2u

Question 9.2

The diagram shows monopolistic competition in the short run with a firm making losses. Explain, using the diagram, how this firm's position would change in the long run if other loss-making firms left the industry.

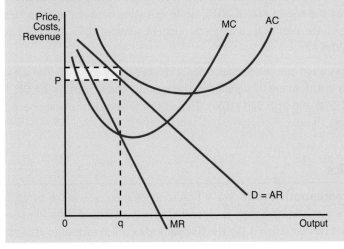

Unit 10: **Oligopoly**

Oligopoly occurs when a few firms between them share a large proportion of the output or sales. Oligopolistic markets have high levels of market concentration. Some oligopolies produce identical products (e.g. metals, sugar or cement) but most produce differentiated products (e.g. cars, soap powder and cigarettes). If the product is identical/homogeneous between firms then price competition or possibly a price fixing cartel is likely. With differentiated products non-price competition is likely with firms using advertising, loyalty cards, packaging and brand proliferation as the main means of increasing market share at the expense of their competitors. A special case of oligopoly is **duopoly** which in its purest form means that only two producers exist in a market. In practice this definition can be relaxed when two firms dominate a market controlling a significant market share between them. There are two duopoly models Cournot and Bertrand. The Cournot model states that the two firms assume each other's output, treat this as a fixed amount and produce accordingly. In the Bertrand model each firm assumes that the other will not change prices in response to price cuts. When both firms use this logic in their strategies they will reach **Nash equilibrium**. Examples of duopoly in the real world include; Pepsi and Coca-Cola, aircraft manufacturers Airbus and Boeing and auctioneers Sotheby's and Christie's. However, duopolies can exist in market segments, for example British Airways competed with BMI on the London Heathrow Manchester/Edinburgh/Aberdeen routes but BMI was taken over by British Airways parent company IAG in 2012. In its place Virgin briefly competed on these routes but by 2015 the duopoly had become a monopoly after Virgin announced its withdrawal of their services with this statement in 2014.

> "Virgin Little Red was launched in March 2013 as an attempt to reintroduce consumer choice on key domestic services after British Airways' takeover of BMI gifted them a monopoly on these routes. Virgin Atlantic has announced its intention to cease its Little Red operation next year. Its daily services between London Heathrow and Manchester will continue until the end of March 2015, while its flights between London Heathrow and Edinburgh and Aberdeen will continue throughout summer 2015 with the final flights in September 2015."

Duopolies result in price and non-price competition and occasionally collusion. The salt which local councils spread on icy roads in the winter is supplied in the main by three firms in the UK, Salt Union (50%), Cleveland Potash (35%) and Irish Salt (10%). Three firms selling such a homogeneous product makes collusion a possibility.

Market characteristics

1. A high market **concentration ratio** (the x-firm concentration ratio is the percentage of the market supplied by the largest x firms). Supply is concentrated in the hands of a few firms (see Unit 3). A better measure of market concentration is the **Herfindahl Index** which takes into account all the firms in an industry and their relative size distribution. The Herfindahl Index involves squaring the market shares of all the firms and then adding them together. A firm with a 20% market share would involve squaring 0.2. The final result will be between 0 and 1 and the nearer the result is to 1 the closer the market is to a monopoly. The index can also produce a result ranging up to 10,000 if the actual market share is used. Hence a duopoly with 50% each would give a Herfindahl Index of 2,500 + 2,500 = 5,000.

2. Firms are interdependent. With so few firms in the market, the actions of one firm will affect the other firms directly.

3. Barriers to entry and exit exist.

Because of the high degree of **interdependence**, oligopoly is a difficult market structure to analyse. The actions of a firm are determined not just by the actions of its rivals but also by the assumptions it makes about its rivals' possible reactions to its own initiatives.

Sweezy's theory of kinked demand

The assumptions of this theory help explain a tendency towards price rigidity often observed in oligopolistic markets. The theory assumes that any firm cutting its price is unlikely to enjoy much of a boost to demand as competitors will follow suit, while any firm raising its price will suffer a great loss of business as competitors are unlikely to follow. Thus the demand curve is kinked at the current price level, being elastic at higher prices and inelastic at lower prices. The firm then has no incentive to change price, and the vertical discontinuity produced in the MR curve by the kink in the AR curve offers a second explanation of price stability. The cost structure of the firm could change radically (MC1 → MC2) without a change in the profit maximising price.

Criticism's of Sweezy's theory include the lack of an explanation as to how the price reached its current level. The standard neo-classical short run profit maximising assumption, employed by Sweezy, is also questioned. However, a longer term view of profit maximisation (entailing a policy such as cost plus pricing) might also result in price stability (see Unit 5).

Figure 10.1: Sweezy's kinked demand curve

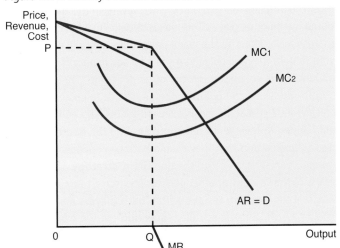

Game theory

In recent years game theory has become a popular way of examining the strategies that oligopolists may adopt in a market. When game theory is applied to oligopoly the players are firms, the game is played in the market, their strategies are their price/output decisions and the payoffs are their profits. Game theory involves studying the alternative strategies oligopolists may choose to adopt depending on their assumptions about their rivals' behaviour. Put at its simplest, if a firm is considering reducing its price, in making its decision it will need to take into account how its rival oligopolists might react and how it will affect them. Firms can choose high risk or low risk strategies in what is very similar to a game of poker between four or five players or chess between two players. The problem for firms is that they have imperfect knowledge of other firms' actions and reactions.

Firms can choose high risk or low risk strategies in what is very similar to a game of chess.

The simplest way of explaining game theory is through the **Prisoner's dilemma**. Suppose two criminals, Bill and Fred have been caught by the police who have enough evidence to get a conviction for some minor offences which would get both prisoners a 4 year jail term. The police think the two have also committed a much more serious crime but don't have enough evidence to charge them. The only way the police could get this evidence is by one of the two confessing to the more serious crime. Bill and Fred are put in separate cells to be interviewed. What is the best strategy each could adopt assuming they cannot trust each other?

Fred

	Confess	Not Confess
Confess	8 / 8	15 / 2
Not Confess	2 / 15	4 / 4

(Bill = rows; in each cell Bill's payoff is lower-left, Fred's payoff is upper-right)

The matrix above shows the options that are available to Bill and Fred and the pay-offs in terms of years in prison each would face. The problem for each of the two 'players' in this game is that they are unsure of the strategy being adopted by the other player. This makes decision making difficult and uncertain as they cannot collude. If both prisoners confess to the major crime then they will each get 8 years. If they both say nothing and refuse to confess they will only get 4 years for the minor offences the police have enough evidence for. What happens if one confesses and the other does not? The confession will implicate the prisoner who has not confessed giving the police enough evidence to convict them both. For example if Bill confesses he only receives a 2 year sentence as a reward for his help and Fred gets 15 years for being obstructive. This would happen in reverse if Fred confesses and Bill doesn't. What would be the best strategy for Bill and Fred? The answer is that they should both confess because the worst they could get is 8 years and the best only 2 years. This is called the **dominant strategy** which is the best strategy for a player in a game regardless of the strategy of other players. The top left box in the above matrix is also the **Nash Equilibrium** which is the position resulting from both players making their optimal decision, maximising their minimum pay-off, sometimes called '**maximin**'. In the world of the Prisoner's dilemma the two prisoners could not collude once they had been arrested, but in the world of business firms can and will as this is the profit maximising outcome.

In the table below firms X and Y are both selling their product in a duopolistic market for £1 and are separately thinking of cutting their prices to 80p. At £1 each firm makes a profit of £6m. Looking at firm X, if it left its price at £1 and Y cut its price to 80p then its profits would fall to £3.5m and Y's would rise to £7m. Alternatively if it cut its price to 80p and Y left its price at £1 then X's profits would rise to £7m. Both firms know that the other is thinking through the same strategies and so they both cut price to 80p and thus make £5m profit. This rational strategy poses the least risk and uncertainty for the two firms. If either left their price at £1, profits for either firm could fall to £3.5m. Clearly the option of collusion exists which gives them a chance of higher profits with price fixed at £1 by agreement or possibly by **tacit collusion**.

Firm X's price

Firm Y's price	£1	80p
£1	£6m each	£3.5m Y £7m X
80p	£7m Y £3.5m X	£5m each

Game theory suggests that firms don't trust each other and in the above matrix the two firms end up setting a price of 80p by attempting independently to choose their best strategy whatever the other firm's strategies could be. This is the **Nash Equilibrium**, which is a situation in which the firms interacting with one another each choose their best strategy given the strategies that all the other firms have chosen. A game may have many Nash equilibria or none at all.

Game theory was used by the UK government in 2000 when it raised £22.5bn from the telephone companies in an auction for the 3G mobile phone licences, which deliver voice, fax and video.

The auction took place in a sequence of rounds, with bids submitted by fax. In each round, participants bid simultaneously for any one of the five licences – with Licence A reserved for new entrants. At the end of each round, bidders were informed of all bids. The holder of the highest bid on each licence was required to remain inactive in following rounds until outbid. The auction ended when no more bids were received.

Thirteen firms started in the auction – the four existing mobile operators and nine potential new entrants. The top bidders after 126 rounds were Licence A, TIW, £4.1bn; Licence B, Vodafone, £5.1bn; Licence C, BT3G, £3.4bn; Licence D, One2One, £3.4bn; Licence E, Orange, £3.6bn. The four large existing operators, Vodafone, BT Cellnet, One2One and Orange led the bidding. Vodafone and BT's networks were overstretched and needed more capacity in order to get more customers, and thus they had to get one of the licences. The result was the phone companies paying much more than was expected for these licences which benefited the government and the tax payer.

In 2012 Ofcom (the telecommunications and media regulator) outlined plans for the auction of the valuable broadcast transmission spectrum that will be freed up by turning off the analogue television signal. The spectrum will be suitable for services such as ultra-fast wireless broadband and more digital terrestrial TV channels. In 2013 this 4G auction raised £2.4bn for the government. Firms such as Dot Econ (http://www.dotecon.com) advise government and regulators such as Ofcom on how to conduct auctions of this kind. According to its web site: "Regulators now use auctions for divestments and DotEcon provides a one-stop shop for all aspects of designing and running auctions. Implementing an auction requires a wide range of skills particularly the use of **game theory** to understand how the auction design affects incentives."

A **zero sum game** is one which whatever is won by one player/firm is lost by another. Such a strategy, which allows one firm to gain, must mean that another firm must lose. Some economists have argued that brand promotion by firms is a zero sum game. Special promotions and in-store displays can boost the sales of individual brands but overall total sales from all brands do not increase. The increased sales from the brands on promotion are taken from other brands that are not.

To compete or collude? Pricing strategy under oligopoly

If and when price stability under conditions of oligopoly breaks down, **price wars** frequently result (as illustrated by intense price competition with petrol retailing and air travel). The retail petrol market has seen a number of such wars over the past two decades. It is in part because of the fear of price wars that oligopoly tends to be characterised by various forms of non-price competition.

It is often observed that oligopolistic firms are torn between two conflicting desires: the wish to compete on one hand, and the wish to collude on the other. The hope of winning any price war tempts some firms (particularly those with significant advantages, such as lower costs) but collusion is an attractive proposition given the desire to remove the uncomfortable uncertainty that interdependence brings to the market. Collusion reduces the fear of competitive price-cutting or retaliatory advertising, which could reduce industry profits.

(a) Collusion in oligopoly

Where oligopolists agree formally or informally to limit competition between themselves they may set output quotas, fix prices, or limit product promotion or development or even agree not to poach each other's markets.

A formal covert collusive agreement is called a **cartel**. A cartel can achieve the same profits as if the industry were a monopoly. In the left hand diagram of Figure 10.2 the total market or industry demand curve is shown as D and the corresponding marginal revenue curve is MR. The cartel's marginal cost curve (MC) is the horizontal sum of the marginal cost curves of the members of the cartel. The cartel will set a price of p1 (MC = MR) where profits are maximised. Alternatively the cartel could set output at q1 by giving each cartel member an output quota. This would produce the same price (p1). A cartel member's quota is shown as qx

in the right hand diagram in Figure 10.2. This enables a cartel member to make abnormal profit shown by the shaded area. The cartel member might be tempted to cheat and raise output to where price = MC. If this was not discovered then profits would be even higher than if they stuck to the agreed quota.

By contrast, p2 shows the marginal cost price, which would be the price under perfect competition, with q2 showing the corresponding output. This means that the cartel will operate with a higher price and lower output when compared to perfect competition. The effect of the cartel is to reduce the consumer surplus and increase the producer surplus and create a **deadweight welfare loss** (shaded in the left hand diagram below).

Figure 10.2: Cartel with a monopoly price

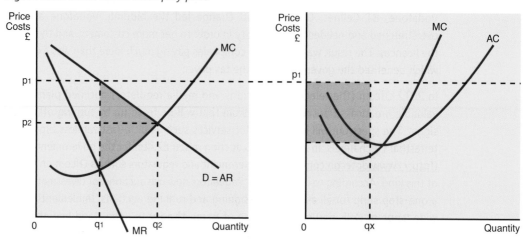

Covert collusion occurs where firms meet secretly and make decisions about prices or output. **Overt** collusive agreements are publicly made and are usually global in nature applying to particular commodities. OPEC, a group of petroleum exporting countries, sets production quotas for member countries to regulate the world price of oil. **Tacit collusion** is much more difficult to control. This is when firms act as if they have common pricing and output policies in place without actually having communicated with each other.

Evidence of tacit collusion is seen when seemingly independent but parallel actions occur among supposedly competing oligopolists. These actions include raising prices which lead to higher profits for the firms. The outcome of this implicit collusion is the same as if there had been explicit agreement between the firms. The fact that there has been no formal agreement makes it more difficult for the competition authorities to punish the firms involved. Tacit collusion is associated with **price leadership** and **complex monopoly**.

Collusion between firms whether formal or informal is more likely when:

● there are only a few firms in the industry, so reaching an agreement is easier and any cheating can be spotted quickly.

● they have similar costs of production and methods of production making any agreement on price easier to reach.

● the firms produce homogeneous products where product differentiation is not a feature of the market. It is thus not surprising that cartels have been found in industries such as cement and heating oil in recent years. The EU competition authorities have dealt with EU-wide cartels in both glass, synthetic rubber and cement in recent years.

● the products have price inelastic demand meaning that a rise in price by the cartel will lead to a rise in sales revenue for the firms.

● collusive agreements are more likely to succeed when total industry demand is stable and where pricing and output decisions are public making cheating easier to detect.

● the laws against collusion in a country are weak or ineffective. In the United States and the European Union the powers and punishments which can be imposed by regulators have been strengthened in recent years. In 2010 the European Union Competition Commission fined 11 air cargo carriers a total of €799m for operating a worldwide cartel which affected cargo services within the European Union.

Collusive agreements often prove difficult to sustain. Most are illegal as they raise prices to the detriment of the consumer. They cannot, therefore, be enforced by contract, even if cheating could be detected. Each and every party to the collusive agreement has an incentive to cheat by producing more than agreed. This will suppress price slightly, but the firm can still take advantage of artificially high prices as long as the other firms do not cheat as well. However, stable market conditions (a small number of firms; similar costs of production; similar products; high barriers to entry; easy detection of cheating on the agreement) make joint profit maximisation feasible. The incentive to cheat among colluding firms can be assessed using game theory.

Most collusive agreements are illegal as they raise prices to the detriment of the consumer.

Cartels often have a limited life and there are many possible reasons for them breaking down. There is always a temptation for firms to increase their output above their quota to gain extra revenue – cheating by cartel members is common. In addition the entry of new firms into the market can undermine the cartel as non-cartel members sell their products at a price below those of cartel members. Increased powers of regulators such as the Competition and Markets Authority and the European Competition Commission have also made it difficult for cartel members to maintain agreements long term.

(i) Price leadership (dominant firm model)

One form of tacit collusion is where firms set the same price as an established price leader. The price leader is usually the 'dominant firm' in the market, this position being achieved through some factor such as size or cost advantage. A dominant firm usually has around a 40% market share.

Figure 10.3 illustrates the dominant firm model. The dominant firm sets the price and then allows the other firms to supply as much as they wish at this price. The dominant firm supplies the remaining, or residual, market demand. This behaviour offers all firms the advantage of certainty; the dominant firm is able to set the price, while the remaining firms know that they will be able to supply as much as they wish at the price set.

Figure 10.3: The dominant firm model

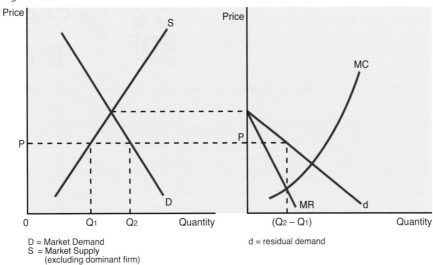

D = Market Demand
S = Market Supply
   (excluding dominant firm)

d = residual demand

Another way of illustrating the dominant firm model is to return to the kinked demand curve as shown in Figure 10.4. The dominant firm is a low cost producer with marginal costs of MC_1; a high cost rival firm would have higher marginal costs (MC_2). The latter firm would like to charge a higher price than the

dominant firm to maximise its profits but has to accept the profit maximising price set by the dominant firm who would not follow any price rise. The lower costs of the dominant firm would mean that a higher cost producer could not win a price war if it tried to cut the price set by the dominant firm at the kink.

Hence there is an identical price across the industry but this price favours the dominant firm.

Figure 10.4

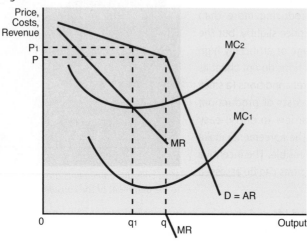

(ii) Price leadership (barometric)

This occurs when a price change by one firm in an oligopoly as a result of changes in the macroeconomic environment (a recession) or market conditions in the industry (a change in demand or input costs) results in all the other firms in the industry changing their prices by the same amount. Many analysts argued that this has occurred in the UK energy sector in recent years when gas and electricity rose and fell by very similar amounts. If the firms have similar cost structures and maintain similar mark-ups this form of price leadership seems quite plausible especially if the product is homogeneous such as gas and electricity.

Consumer pressure groups such as 'Which?' have often felt that the UK energy **oligopoly** (the Big Six) has been keen to pass on rising wholesale energy costs to customers in higher bills, but less enthusiastic to do so when they are falling. There have been many that have felt the energy market is rigged against consumers and the Labour Party Opposition in 2015 vowed to freeze gas and electricity bills until 2017 had they won the election.

Many feel that **tacit collusion** is present in this market although customers themselves have often failed to make the effort to take advantage of cheaper energy deals by investigating different suppliers. This is called **customer inertia**. However, at the same time many household and business energy users have been confused by the complex opaque pricing structure used by the energy companies. An investigation by the regulator Ofgem said that the whole market needed to be simplified and suppliers must provide one, comparable, unit rate price giving greater transparency for consumers. Ofgem felt for some time that there was weak competition in the energy market with the Big Six companies supplying energy to 95% of UK households. Price announcements from the Big Six were often at the same time and the magnitude of the price changes were often the same. The regulator felt that there may not have been a cartel but tacit collusion was more than likely. In 2014 Ofgem referred the energy market for a full investigation by the Competition and Markets Authority. One of their preliminary findings was as follows:

> "We have noted that there is a wide variation in the prices that different domestic customers pay for energy, which is particularly striking since electricity and gas are entirely homogenous products. We calculate that, over the period from 2012 to 2014, most customers of the Six Large Energy Firms could have made considerable savings from switching a combination of suppliers, tariffs and payment methods."

(iii) Complex monopolies

A complex monopoly is said to exist when a market is served by at least two firms which are not interconnected who engage in conduct, whether by collusion or not, which is likely to restrict, distort or prevent competition. The firms in question would have to control at least 25% of the market for the public interest to be damaged though (sometimes called a working monopoly). The firms, although pursuing individual non-collusive policies, behave in a uniform manner resulting in a situation, which appears as though they have colluded. In recent years the UK competition authorities found that the major supermarkets and the big commercial banks belong to complex monopolies. The UK's cement market, arguably a complex monopoly, has had to take measures to enhance competition in this industry following changes ordered by the Competition Commission. The UK Competition Commission (now the Competition and Markets Authority) spent two years studying the UK cement market and reported in 2014 that firms were prioritising the preservation of their market share and failing to compete effectively. The Commission found that the lack of competition was costing cement users in the building and construction industry £30m a year. The Commission ordered one of the dominant firms Lafarge Tarmac to sell one of two cement plants and Hanson, another firm with a large market share, to sell one of its ground granulated blast furnace slag plants so as to remedy perceived 'adverse effects on competition' caused by the concentrated structure of those markets.

Can collusion ever be in the public interest?

In theory a price fixing cartel will reduce the consumer surplus, increase the producer surplus and bring about a welfare loss. However, it has been argued that in certain circumstances a cartel produces industry wide benefits that are arguably in the public interest. For example many have applauded the collective selling of television rights for coverage of sport. In 2005 the European Union (EU) Competition Commission initially felt that the FA Premier League of 20 clubs was against the public interest as it is a cartel. However, it can be argued that such collective selling protects the smaller clubs in the Premier League and brings more money into football than if the clubs each negotiated their own television deals in an open competitive market. In other parts of Europe clubs were able for some time to negotiate their own television deals with broadcasters but this penalised smaller clubs whose revenues would be much lower as their games generated less interest. Put simply the Premier League cartel protects clubs such as Stoke City and West Bromwich Albion who would otherwise struggle to gain much television revenue when they played each other. While Manchester United versus Chelsea would generate a lucrative broadcasting fee. Cartels tend to protect their weakest members and in the case of the Premier League it is the less glamorous clubs.

Recent television deals negotiated between the FA Premier League and television broadcasters include a European Competition Commission stipulation that the League cannot sell all their television rights to one buyer, which in the past had been BSkyB. From the start of the 2016-17 season 168 matches will be shown live. Sky recently paid £4.2bn for five of the seven TV packages while rival BT paid £960m for the other two in the record TV rights auction. The deal runs for three years from 2016 to 2019. Thus while the Premier League acts as a monopoly seller of television rights there is no longer a sole buyer of these rights. However Virgin Media were not happy with the bidding process and submitted a complaint to the regulator Ofcom. Virgin stated that "The rapidly rising cost of Premier League live broadcast rights means UK fans pay the highest prices in Europe to watch football on TV." The company's complaint to the regulator highlights differences between the way Premier League rights are sold and the way broadcasters bid to show matches in France, Germany, Italy and Spain.

All the European leagues allow broadcasters to show every top flight match to be broadcast live, while the Premier League sold rights to only 168 of 380 matches per season at its last auction. Virgin Media believed that selling rights to more games per season would mean better value for money for television viewers. High prices and a restriction of supply are common features of a cartel.

The same principle has been argued in relation to Britain's 60 racecourses that have collectively sold their television rights. Racing UK is a subscription-only television channel which broadcasts horse racing from 34 UK courses. These courses are effectively the owners of the channel which was launched in 2004 – after racecourses were given the freedom to collectively negotiate their own broadcasting rights. The other 26 UK race courses broadcast their races on At The Races channel.

It is important to distinguish collusion from co-operation by firms or **joint ventures**. The strategic airline alliances such as 'One World', 'Star Alliance' and 'SkyTeam' arguably benefit the long haul traveller as well as the airlines by producing lower costs. The advantages of these alliances for the airlines are an extended network through sharing the same flight code. There are also potential cost reductions through the sharing of sales offices, maintenance facilities, computer systems and check in facilities. Clearly these alliances have helped to keep costs lower in the battle with budget airlines although some argue that these alliances give significantly more advantages to the airlines than the traveller. As in theory the airlines have not exchanged commercially sensitive information they are not seen to be acting anti-competitively. Motor manufacturers have often co-operated in the high cost and high risk areas of product development, e.g. fuel cell technology. The Eurofighter is also a co-operative venture of three companies: Alenia Aermacchi, Airbus Group and BAE Systems.

(b) Competitive pricing

(i) Entry limit pricing (limit pricing)

This policy entails charging the highest price compatible with deterring new entry to the market. The price is set below the profit maximising level, because of the fear that this price will be sufficiently high to attract new firms into the market. Limit pricing is discussed in more detail in Unit 11.

(ii) Predatory pricing

A predatory pricing policy is designed to force competitors out of the market. If a firm believes that it can sustain a very low price for longer than its rivals, it might charge such a price on a temporary basis. Usually the predator will set a price below average variable cost. When the target of the policy has been forced out of business, the predator will then raise its price to the profit maximising level. Such policies constitute an anti-competitive practice and are therefore outlawed by UK competition law (see Unit 15).

In the past large bus companies in the UK have been accused of predatory pricing. They allegedly used the profits made from high fares on routes where they faced no competition to subsidise very low fares on routes where they faced competition from small operators. By setting fares below average variable costs the larger operators could drive the new entrants out of the market. When Stelios Haji-Ioannou launched easyBus in 2004 he accused National Express, a well established operator, of predatory pricing on his Milton Keynes to London route.

In 2005 Tesco was accused of predatory pricing by the Association of Convenience Stores. Increasingly Tesco and Sainsbury are opening small grocery outlets to serve a local community (Tesco Express). Independent grocery stores have traditionally served this market. In 2005 a small Tesco opened in Withernsea, an East Yorkshire town, and sent 6,000 households £8 discount vouchers if £20 was spent in the local Tesco store. This was the equivalent of a 40% discount. It has been alleged that this was predatory pricing designed to force small grocers out of the market. In recent years small independently owned petrol stations have objected to planning application by supermarkets such as Tesco claiming that they often use a 'predatory' pricing policy of selling fuel below cost to get people into the supermarket to buy groceries but often raising the price once the local petrol retail competition had been eliminated. However such activities have to be sustained for a period of time before the competition authorities can take action.

The issue of predatory pricing has been raised in recent years with the revolution in taxi services brought about by Uber. Uber has turned the process of booking a taxi on its head in many cities around the world. A mobile phone app allows a customer to check for cars in the area, book one with a click, and have it charged – usually at a cheaper price than a traditional taxi – to a credit card.

In London the traditional black cabs bear greater costs as they are subject to more regulation, although this allows them to pick up anyone from the street. In contrast, private hire vehicles such as Uber are subject to less regulation because they are booked in advance. Uber enjoys a significant price advantage by not paying UK corporation tax, because customers, via their app, are booked through the Netherlands. Despite Uber being a $50bn (£32bn) company, its drivers earn far less than the London living wage and in some cases, they earn a lot less than the minimum wage. Many critics of Uber argue that the low prices offered by the app based company are kept artificially low to drive out competition — which is predatory pricing.

The number of minicab drivers in London has increased by 46 per cent to 86,500 compared to five years ago and is increasing by 1,000 every month, and there is pressure for the Competition and Markets Authority to investigate the London taxi market as a whole.

How does a regulator distinguish predatory pricing from a price war which is just an extreme form of price competition? The European Union competition rules which are used to judge to test for predatory pricing are as follows:

● Prices set below average variable cost by a dominant firm will always be assumed to be abusive and anti-competitive.

● Prices set below average cost but above average variable cost will be regarded as abusive and anti-competitive if they are part of a plan to dominate a market and eliminate competitors.

(iii) Marginal cost pricing

This pricing policy is most likely in industries in public ownership or in industries in private hands, which are being regulated by a government agency.

Such pricing maximises consumer welfare and leads to an optimum allocation of resources. Consumers pay a price, the valuation they place upon the product, that is equal to the cost of producing one extra unit of output, the resource cost (i.e. price = marginal cost which is allocatively efficient).

Figure 10.5(i): Marginal cost pricing

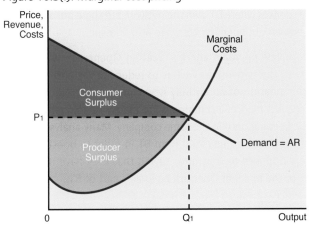

At price OP_1 in Figure 10.5(i), the industry is to supply output OQ_1 and the community surplus is maximised. (The benefits obtained by both consumers and producers – but not paid for.) This is said to be the output level that maximises social benefit. If marginal cost pricing is abandoned as in Figure 10.5(ii) and the price reverts to a profit maximising price, the shaded area represents the **deadweight welfare loss** of such a price change.

Figure 10.5(ii)

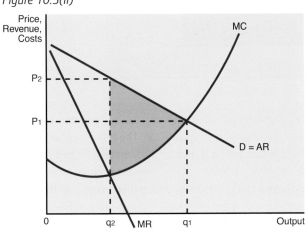

Practical difficulties in marginal cost pricing

1. MC pricing fails to take into account changes in demand, particularly for gas, electricity, transport and telecommunications, where demand varies daily, weekly and from season to season.

   For example, commuter trains are crowded during the 'rush hour' but have few passengers for the rest of the day; at peak periods, to carry one extra passenger may require an extra train service, whilst, at off-peak periods, the marginal cost of carrying an extra passenger is virtually zero. Such variations in demand make it very hard to estimate marginal cost realistically.

2. In integrated systems of production, such as the electricity industry, marginal cost is very hard to identify. For example, an increase in the price of gas which raises the MC of generating electricity in gas-fired power stations by say 10% does not enable the industry to increase price by exactly 10%. This is because a single consumer, through the grid system, might be consuming electricity generated in nuclear or coal-fired power stations where marginal costs are unchanged. The problem facing the industry is to estimate the overall increase in the marginal cost of the system. '**Unbundling**' the costs in such a complex market is thus very difficult, and poses a problem for regulators.

   To understand 'unbundling' think of a food hamper you may receive from a department store. If you want to unbundle the cost of the hamper you need to find the price of each item of food in the hamper by visiting the store. In an industry the unbundling of costs is the process of identifying each distinct aspect of the provision of a product or service and determining its cost. It can be used in the regulation of privatised utilities such as electricity supply which is sub-divided into generation, transmission, and distribution. In telephone services where BT own the network but there are other providers to consumers who need to access this network unbundling costs are also an issue.

   BT unbundled its network several years ago by creating Openreach which was designed to give competitors easier access to the network as well as to reduce prices and avoid wasteful duplication. However, this was not the creation of an entirely new company like Network Rail or National Grid. Instead the regulator Ofcom decided as a compromise to merely functionally separate the retail part of BT from the network while keeping both in the same company. Many analysts now believe that this was a mistake and want Openreach to be demerged from BT in order to boost investment and quality of service. Predictably BT are opposed to this move saying that they have invested significantly in the network in recent years. For the moment Openreach remains part of BT.

   Figure 10.6: Losses with marginal cost pricing

   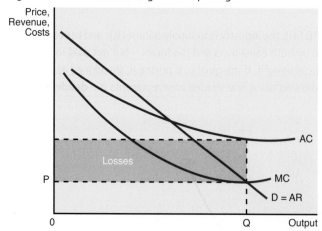

3. Marginal cost pricing may cause an industry with decreasing long-run costs (a national monopoly perhaps) to encounter financial deficits (see Figure 10.6). The loss arises because the enterprise charges a price below long-run average cost and so is unable to generate sufficient revenue to replace worn out equipment and plant. This applies particularly to businesses such as railways which have decreasing long-run costs with an extensive track, signaling, and stations network. If marginal cost pricing were applied to household consumers of water who were using a metering system, then a standing fixed charge would have to be applied to cover the high fixed costs of pipeline and drainage systems that are

needed in water infrastructure. In these declining cost industries marginal cost pricing does not cover the full cost of provision. Figure 10.7 does show that marginal cost pricing can give a firm abnormal profits in some circumstances.

4. The marginal cost-pricing rule is designed to achieve **Pareto efficiency** in the allocation of resources (see Unit 12). But, when there are externalities, this should be incorporated into the estimates of marginal costs and benefits.

5. If marginal costs are rising sharply and demand is high the firm will make abnormal profits, as can be seen in Figure 10.7.

Figure 10.7: Abnormal profits with marginal cost pricing

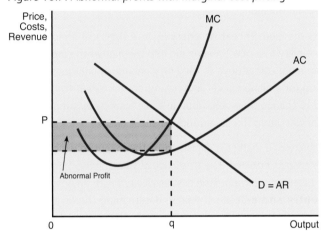

Non-price competition

This can take a variety of forms including product differentiation, product development, loyalty cards and sales promotion. The policies have three broad aims: expanding the total market; expanding the individual firm's share of the existing market; and fostering brand loyalty which will make the firm's demand less price elastic. A successful advertising campaign will shift the demand curve to the right and decrease elasticity. Consumers' brand loyalty will thus make them less sensitive to price changes. In recent years retailers, especially supermarkets, to build brand loyalty, have used loyalty cards such as Nectar and Tesco Clubcard extensively. Buyers of petrol may go to BP regularly to collect Nectar points when petrol may be cheaper elsewhere. Newspapers have also used free DVDs, CDs and posters to entice people to buy a copy of their latest edition. Such non-price competition tends to reduce the risk of price competition, which can sometimes lead to a damaging price war.

Question 10.1

What are the potential advantages of collusion to consumers?

Question 10.2

What are the advantages and disadvantages of airline alliances such as Star Alliance to air passengers?

Unit 11: **Contestable markets theory**

Amongst the chief determinants of a firm's behaviour, according to neo-classical theory, is the number and size of its competitors. The key insight offered by its relatively new 'rival', the contestable markets approach is that *potential* competitors (not yet in existence, or at least not operating in this market) can have an important influence on the conduct of the firm. The theory came to prominence in the early 1980s, largely through the work of William Baumol.

Clearly in many markets the mere **threat of entry** by new firms will affect the behaviour of incumbent firms. If there is the possibility of a new firm coming into the market the incumbent firms may respond by cutting costs to become more competitive or they may engage in limit pricing. If the potential entrant is very small, maybe aiming for a niche market and posing no real threat to the established firms the latter may not have any need to change their behaviour. In some markets existing firms may always behave as if there is a threat of entry whether a threat currently exists or not.

The degree of contestability of a market is measured by the extent to which the gains from market entry for a firm exceeds the cost of entering (i.e. the cost of overcoming barriers to entry), with the risks associated with failure taken into account (the cost associated with any barriers to exit). Accordingly, the levels of **barriers to entry and exit** are crucial in determining the level of a market's contestability. Barriers to exit consist of **sunk costs**, that is to say costs that cannot be recovered when leaving the market. The contestable markets approach suggests that potential entrants consider post-entry profit levels, rather than the pre-entry levels suggested by neo-classical theory.

In theory perfect competition is a perfectly contestable market and in between that and blockaded entry are varying degrees of contestability. Monopolistic competition has minimal entry barriers although small firms need to build up a customer base and meet certain government regulations. Oligopolies tend to be much less contestable with high capital expenditure and advertising costs to name but two entry barriers. **Blockaded entry** arises when a firm is protected by a legal monopoly, which applies to Camelot which has been the sole licence holder of the National Lottery since it was set up in 1994. The National Lottery Commission (which is now merged with the Gambling Commission) is responsible for awarding a single licence to a commercial operator to run the National Lottery for the benefit of the nation. Camelot were given a ten year renewal to their licence in 2009 but this has since been given a four year extension to 2023. It can also occur when a firm has the protection of a patent, which gives the producer the intellectual property rights to be a legal monopolist for a limited time period.

Obviously no market is perfectly contestable, i.e. with zero sunk costs. In modern economies it is the degree of contestability which is relevant as some markets are more contestable than others. Also just because there have been no new entrants to a market over a given period of time does not mean that this market is not contestable. The threat of entry will be enough to make the existing (incumbent) firms behave in such a way as to recognise this, i.e. by setting a price which doesn't attract entry and which only makes normal profits.

In Figure 11.1 a monopolist is making abnormal profits (shown by the coloured area) in a perfectly contestable market. If there are no entry or exit barriers new firms will enter the market attracted by the high profits. The monopolist is then forced to reduce price to P2 where sales volume is maximised and normal profits are earned (AC = AR), when trying to assess the contestability of a market. Technological change can make a market more contestable e.g. the internet has allowed new firms into many markets. Some markets are less contestable because of the high level of expenditure on such things as infrastructure e.g. water pipelines, where very strong brands exist in a market, or where new entrants will have to spend heavily on advertising. Witness the ultimately futile attempt by ITV Digital in 2001 to break into the market for pay TV where Sky was an established brand. The failure of ITV (a huge established broadcaster) is in stark contrast to the initial success of Setanta Sports which was formed only in 1990 as an outlet for Irish sporting events to Irish expatriates. This firm made a successful entry into subscription sports broadcasting helped partly by a European Commission ruling which prevented BSkyB buying the rights to all of the English Premier League's games. However, in 2009 Setanta UK went into administration as the number of subscribers failed to reach the break-even point for survival. In recent years the entry of BT to the pay-to-view football market has established the company as a strong rival to BSkyB, successfully bidding for Premier League broadcasting rights and also winning the right to broadcast the UEFA Champions League matches. However, BT had to spend a lot of money to break into this market and smaller broadcasters don't have their resources. The EU's successful liberalisation of the air transport industry in the 1990s ushered in a period of unprecedented growth in air transport and introduced many new entrants into the market such as budget airlines easyJet and Ryanair with their low cost business models. The growth of the internet for bookings and printing boarding passes further helped these and other airlines enter a market previously dominated by national 'flag carriers' such as British Airways and Lufthansa.

Just the threat of entry of a new firm is enough to impose a constraint on incumbent (existing firms) meaning that that these well-established firms behave as if the market was already highly competitive. A good example from New Zealand also relates to air travel. In 2015 Air New Zealand significantly cut its regional air fares just as budget airline Jetstar prepared to enter the market. Air New Zealand has had dominance of the regional aviation market in the country for many years and fares dropped by up to 40 per cent on dozens of routes ahead of Jetstar's announcement of where it planned to fly in the country.

Well established firms have well developed data bases relating to their customers and suppliers which new entrants will have to build up over time. This **information gap** works against potential entrants who will realise that it takes time to acquire this knowledge. Markets will also be less contestable if the established firms have a reputation for limit pricing, putting off new entrants. This issue is dealt with in the next section.

Figure 11.1: Contestable markets

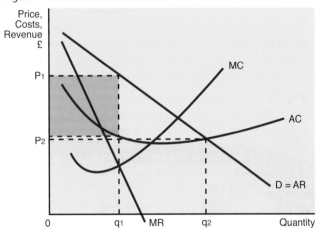

Entry limit pricing (limit pricing)

The fear on the part of existing firms of rendering the market contestable (stimulating new entry) by making high levels of profit is likely to lead to the adoption of entry limit pricing, a concept introduced in the previous unit. This is essentially a defensive strategy, with existing firms setting prices as high as possible but not so high as to enable new-comers to enter the industry. Limit pricing works effectively when the established firms have lower costs than the potential entrant. In the diagram below (Figure 11.2) the long run average costs of the established firms are represented by LRAC1 and the potential entrant's by LRAC2 assuming that the firms face constant costs. When there is no threat of entry the established firm sets its price at a profit maximising P1, but if there is a threat of entry the established firm sets a limit price of PL which is equal to the long run average cost of the potential entrant. Entry by a new firm would add extra production to the industry increasing output beyond qL to say q2. This extra output will depress price to P2 and make entry by the potential entrant unprofitable as the market price would now be below its long run average cost (LRAC2).

Figure 11.2: Entry limit pricing

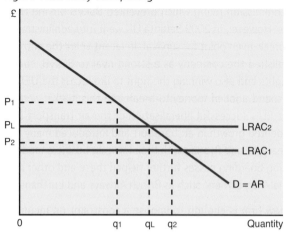

A market with no barriers to entry or exit would be considered perfectly contestable. Entry limit pricing in such a market would entail setting price equal to average cost, so that only normal profits are made. Where barriers to entry and exit exist limit pricing provides scope for supernormal profits to be made; the higher the barriers the higher the profits that can be made by deterring entry. In summary, contestable markets theory predicts that firms might be forced to set price as though operating in a competitive market even in the absence of actual competition. The lower the barriers to entry and exit, the greater the extent to which prices will be set at this level.

If existing firms choose not to adopt entry limit pricing, the potential exists for contestable markets to be highly unstable. Markets, which are highly contestable, are likely to be vulnerable to '**hit and run competition**'. Consider a situation where existing firms are pricing at above the entry-limit level. Even in the event that existing firms react in a predatory style, new entry will be profitable as long as there is a time lag between entry and the implementation of such action. Having made a profit in the intervening period, the new entrant can then leave the market at very little cost. The double-glazing industry is one area that exhibits behaviour compatible with this theory. The market in many regions is dominated by a number of firms that have had a long-term presence in the industry, but who are frequently challenged by new entrants, many of whom leave the market after a short time.

The double-glazing industry is susceptible to 'hit and run competition'.

The order in which firms enter a particular market can have a significant effect on the conduct of firms and the behaviour of customers. The first significant firm to enter a new market is called the first mover. This firm has advantages from this and there are several **first mover advantages**. These include the opportunity for this firm to establish a good reputation and gain brand loyalty possibly making demand for their product price inelastic. Secondly customers who initially buy the first mover's product may find it difficult to switch to the products of subsequent entrants. This is best illustrated with the Apple iPod (a first mover), because any songs downloaded via Apple's iTunes were not able to be transferred to other MP3 players.

Clearly first movers may face disadvantages though. Specifically, later entrants can sometimes copy the technology used by first movers, although the latter will probably have gained some patent protection for this. Late entrants are also able to take advantage of the mistakes made by first movers who are often on a steep learning curve when operating in a new market. These firms may be able to adapt to changing technological and market conditions more effectively than the first mover.

Question 11.1

What factors may have led to the banking sector becoming more contestable in recent years?

Question 11.2

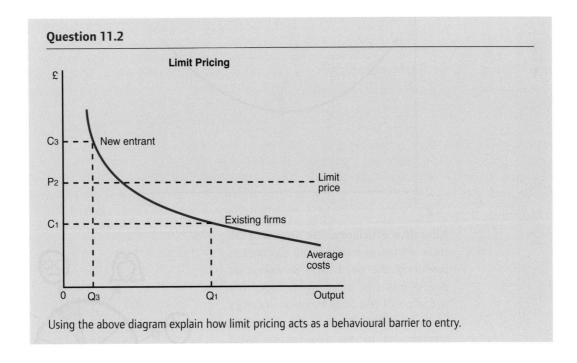

Using the above diagram explain how limit pricing acts as a behavioural barrier to entry.

Unit 12: **Economic efficiency and the conditions necessary for its attainment**

Economic efficiency is concerned with the relationship between production and the scarce inputs used. In other words, how well are resources combined to produce an end result?

1. **Productive efficiency.** This entails operating at the lowest possible average cost of production, and attainment is therefore dependent on reaping all available economies of scale (long run cost savings derived from the size of the firm). See point A on Figure 12.1.

2. **Technical efficiency.** This is achieved when any given output is produced with the minimum quantity of inputs. By implication, any point on the long-run average cost curve, which represents the minimum level of cost for any given output, is technically efficient. Production above the curve is not, the inefficiency involved sometimes being known as **x-inefficiency** (see point B below).

Figure 12.1: Technical and productive efficiency

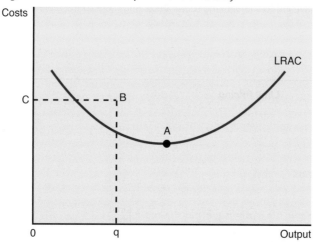

3. **Allocative efficiency.** This deals with the issue of whether resources are allocated to producing the goods and services that people want. In other words, does the allocation of resources maximise society's utility (benefit)? It would, of course, be possible for us to make goods using productively efficient processes yet for no one to want the end product.

The charge of allocative inefficiency was often levelled at centrally planned (command) economies (such as the former Soviet Union), because it is difficult for planners to gauge the public's wishes accurately. An advantage of the market economy is that because firms make profits by satisfying the demands of the consumer, the consumer is sovereign and dictates which goods and services are produced – at least in theory.

Productive and allocative efficiency can be shown using a production possibility frontier.

Allocative efficiency deals with the issue of whether resources are allocated to producing the goods and services that people want.

All points on the frontier are productively efficient but only one point is allocatively efficient reflecting consumer preferences. In Figure 12.2 the economy is producing either pizzas or burgers and the allocatively efficient level of burger production is at q. That position is derived from the diagram below where the marginal social benefit (MPB) intersects with the marginal social cost (MPC). Other levels of production at q1 and q2 are not allocatively efficient. At q1 the MPB is greater than the MPC indicating that more burgers should be produced to increase consumer benefit but at q2 MPC is greater than MPB and thus fewer burgers should be produced.

Figure 12.2: Allocative efficiency

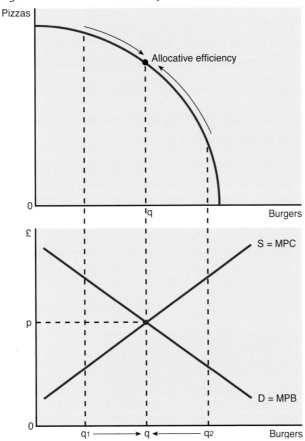

Figure 12.3: Allocative efficiency

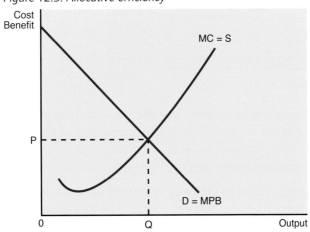

Figure 12.3 depicts the supply curve, drawn on the assumption of a perfectly competitive market, and equal to the marginal cost (MC) of production. The demand curve informs us of the price associated with any given level of demand. This price will equal the marginal private benefit (MPB) or satisfaction derived from the last unit of consumption, as we can expect consumers to demand an extra unit of a product as long as MPB exceeds the cost of consumption (i.e. the price, P): It is only when MPB has

declined to the point where it equals price that no further units will be demanded. Any level of output to the left of Q (the competitive equilibrium output) does not maximise utility net of costs, since here an extra unit of output will add more to utility than costs. To the right of Q, MC exceeds MPB, suggesting that the last unit produced caused a loss of utility net of costs. Consequently, Q must maximise society's net benefit and must be the allocatively efficient output level. Here, MPB is equated to MC; since MPB is in turn equal to price, allocative efficiency is achieved where:

$$P = MC$$

Given that output level Q is the competitive equilibrium level of output, we can conclude that perfectly competitive markets are allocatively efficient.

It should be noted that the P = MC condition does not secure the attainment of allocative efficiency where externalities (costs or benefits that accrue to third parties as a result of the activities of other economic agents) are present. The analysis above assumes the private costs and benefits to be the only costs and benefits to society.

4. **Distributive efficiency.** The goods produced should be distributed precisely to those consumers who need them most and in an equitable way.

5. **Dynamic efficiency.** This is concerned with the efficient allocation of resources over time (see process innovation and product innovation in Unit 14). Dynamic efficiency is concerned with innovation and investment which will reduce the long run average cost curve. Invention in new machines, new technology and more efficient working practices will shift the long run average cost curve from $LRAC_1$ to $LRAC_2$ (Figure 12.4). Obviously improving dynamic efficiency does involve an increase in costs in the short term but the benefits will be seen in the long run. Its attainment is likely to entail investing a substantial quantity of the resources available today, either to improve the capital stock or to further research and development.

Figure 12.4

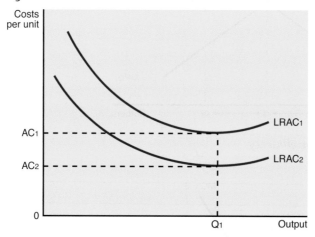

6. **Static efficiency.** Static efficiency measures how efficient a firm or an economy is at a given point in time. It involves the concept of productive efficiency producing at the lowest average cost given existing resources and factor inputs. Static efficiency is also concerned with allocative efficiency, the best distribution of resources in an economy.

In order to establish objective criteria for efficiency, economists often use '**Pareto Efficiency**'. A Pareto efficient allocation of resources is said to exist if it is not possible to reallocate resources so as to improve the well being (or utility) of one person without making at least one person worse off (reduce their utility). The Pareto criterion enables us to assess efficiency but does not say anything about equity. Equity is concerned with fairness and social justice. An efficient economy may be one where the benefits are unfairly shared out and there is a very unequal distribution of income and wealth. For any economy, there are a number of efficient allocations, some of which will involve more equity in distribution between individuals in the society than others. The Pareto criterion cannot distinguish between these.

impose no charges for shrinkage or wastage or shelf positioning. This Code has recently been strengthened by the creation of the Groceries Code Adjudicator to oversee the relationship between supermarkets and their suppliers. It ensures that large supermarkets treat their suppliers lawfully and fairly, investigating complaints and arbitrating in disputes. The adjudicator now has the power to fine any of the top 10 supermarkets up to 1 per cent of their annual turnover for a breach of the Grocery Supply Code of Practice.

The relationship between a supplier and a supermarket is difficult; on the one hand supermarkets are essential clients, but they can also impose crippling costs on their usually smaller suppliers. Possibly with the protection of the Code of Practice and the newly empowered Adjudicator, suppliers may feel more comfortable confronting these large supermarkets. In the past the threat of delisting – termination of supply contracts – has been too severe for most suppliers to take issue with a supermarket over the way they have been treated.

For a number of years many dairy farmers have been affected by the low prices paid for their milk. Most dairy farmers sell their milk to milk processors such as Arla and Dairy Crest who then prepare and bottle it before selling it on to retailers such as supermarkets. In recent years, farmers have seen the price they are paid for their milk fall below their own costs of production and many have left the industry. Figure 13.2 below shows farmers losing 7p per litre on their milk.

Figure 13.2: Approximate cost of a 2 litre bottle of milk

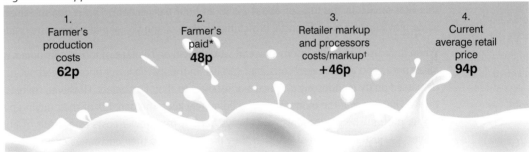

Source: AHDB, NFU, RABDB. *Equivalent to 24p/litre average, August 2015. †Some retailers pay farmers directly. Example figures only, which may vary.

The number of dairy farmers in the UK was estimated to be 25,000 in 2000 but by the end of 2014 the number had dipped below 10,000 for the first time. Dairy farming is rather like perfect competition, many producers selling a homogenous product and unable to influence the market price i.e. they are price takers. Often the low price has been blamed on the supermarkets who use their enormous buying power to enable milk to be used as a loss leader in price wars with their rivals. In 2014 a two litre carton of milk was being sold in some supermarkets for only £1, way below the farmers' cost of production. Milk was being sold for a price below that of bottled water!

However, this is not always a simple abuse of monopsony power by the supermarkets as there has for some time been a massive over supply of milk in Europe pushing prices down. In recent years in response to public pressure a number of supermarkets have now negotiated their own contracts with dairy farmers which give the producers a much fairer price. In addition by 2015 some supermarkets also agreed to pay a minimum price of 28p per litre for milk, although the cost of production for farmers was 30p per litre. The minimum price is actually paid to the milk processors not the dairy farmers, thus there is a question mark over how much they will receive of it. The complex supply chain issues which operate in this industry (liquid milk is used for cream, butter, cheese and yoghurts) make this a difficult problem to solve.

The problem of monopsony power has also arisen in the care home market for the elderly as a result of the buying power of the social services departments of the English local authorities. Local authorities finance nursing home care to those who cannot afford it and as a result block purchase a significant amount of the capacity in the care home sector on behalf of their patients. This buying power has allegedly allowed them to drive down the fees that the care homes can charge to such a low level that many cannot make a profit. Some of these homes charge higher fees to other patients who have the means to pay and who don't use social services (self-funders). This pricing policy allows the homes to survive but is a form of **price discrimination** that is arguably an unfair outcome from the abuse of monopsony power. An interesting

result of this situation has been the emergence of large nursing home groups such as Care UK and Four Seasons who own several care homes. The tendency for powerful sellers to emerge to balance the strength of powerful buyers such as the local authorities is an example of **countervailing power**.

Even the large care home groups have been finding the going tough, as evidenced by the collapse of Southern Cross in 2011. Local authorities and the government are the purchasers of 63% of care home places and at the moment they are not paying the true cost of care which puts enormous strain on the care home sector. As the care home sector is privately owned the businesses are profit motivated and thus the present system is arguably unsustainable.

The problem is inflamed by the local authorities having insufficient funding to pay a true market price for the care home beds they purchase. They may be acting like a monopsonist but it is through necessity rather than greed. In recent years dramatic cuts to social care funding by central government have led the country's largest care providers to join trade unions in warning of potentially large scale closures of care homes. The reduction in fees paid by councils to care providers has played a large part in their worrying financial position. Four Seasons, the UK's biggest care provider which has 20,000 elderly patients across 450 homes reported that its 2014 earnings fell by 32%.

Martin Green, chief executive of Care England, a body which represents independent social care providers, has said: "The population who live in care homes are extremely vulnerable yet the government is funding this vital service to the tune of about £2.50 an hour per resident. This is not sustainable and we will see some providers in severe financial difficulties in the coming years unless this issue is addressed."

When firms use their monopsony power it would seem on the face of it that consumers would gain through lower prices and an increased consumer surplus. In theory the lower prices forced out of their suppliers will be passed on by monopsony producers or retailers to their customers. However, there is no guarantee that this will happen and the monopsonist could merely keep the benefits of their buying power in the form of higher profits. The monopsonist will always benefit from lower costs as a result of abusing their buying power, it is just a question of whether they pass this on to their customers or not.

Employees working for the monopsonist may well gain higher wages as the firm enjoys higher profits, particularly if they receive profit related pay. However, the higher profits gained by a monopsonist may instead be used for investment or paid out in higher dividends to shareholders. Arguably the higher investment might benefit customers through improved quality and in some firms the employees may also own shares and benefit from higher dividends. The monopsonist's suppliers are always likely to be losers as the lower prices they are paid means lower profits, possibly redundancies and maybe exit from the industry. It can be argued that the lower prices being forced on them by monopsonists will pressurise them to reduce their own costs and increase productivity. However, suppliers in general need legal safeguards against abuse of this kind of dominance or they could possibly form selling co-operatives which give them more collective power.

The care home crisis – an abuse of buying power?

Over the next 25 years the number of over 85s in the UK will double and many in this age group will need care either in specialist homes or in their own home. The increased numbers of elderly people will mean another 18,000 needing care home places compared to today. As many as 37,000 care home beds, the equivalent of 1,500 care homes, could be lost by 2020 according to the think tank ResPublica.

Local authorities (mainly county councils) administer adult social care and they purchase beds in care homes on behalf of elderly clients in their jurisdiction. The care home fees are paid by the local authority if clients have low savings, but those with higher savings or with assets such as a house, pay some or all of the fees to the care home. The means tested fees system means that the better off have to pay all of the fees themselves and often have to sell their home to do so. They are said to be 'self funding'.

It seems a little odd that the number of care home beds is going down when the elderly population is increasing. Indeed in January 2011 there were 4,640 delayed discharges of elderly people from NHS hospitals because appropriate care for them could not be arranged. Most of the elderly would like to stay in their own home as long as possible and local authorities support their wishes. Hence, part of the crisis of NHS beds being blocked by the elderly, is the time it takes to arrange what are called packages of care for patients discharged from hospital into their own homes.

It is fair to say that some of the losses in care beds are accounted for by the closure of residential homes resulting from the increased numbers of elderly people continuing to live at home for as long as possible. However, the decline in the number of care home beds is not explained simply by the growth in care provision at home. The fact is making a profit in the privately owned care home sector has become increasingly difficult in recent years. Although there are very large companies in this sector such as Care UK and BUPA Care Homes, who are capable of gaining significant **economies of scale**, even they have struggled. The problem in part is the buying power of local authorities who buy about 60% of beds in care homes on behalf of their clients.

This means that they fix the fees rather than the homes themselves, and care home owners would argue that the fees are not high enough to make a profit. Economists would see the driving down of fees as an abuse of something akin to **monopsony power** by the local authorities. A **monopsonist** is a sole buyer and thus it has huge advantages over the seller. Last April, many local authorities froze the weekly fee per bed leaving care homes with a shortfall/loss on every local authority funded bed of around £90, with £700 the approximate weekly cost per bed. This buying power cannot be explained as an economy of scale where the care homes offer the local authorities discounts for block booking. It seems to be a case of local authorities saying these are our fees - take it or leave it.

Local authorities claim that they have insufficient money to pay any more than they do, although they have recently been given an extra £2bn for adult social care by the central government. However, this money is not ring fenced for care home provision. How do the care homes survive in this situation? Some care homes charge more for self funding clients than they receive for local authority funded clients which in itself is probably anti-competitive and an example of **price discrimination**. There is a possibility of 100,000 elderly people occupying the 170,000 NHS hospital beds in a few years' time if current trends continue. There will simply not be enough care home places to put them when ready for discharge from the NHS hospitals where many are initially admitted. Many would argue that the elderly care problem is too large for the local authorities to handle and that a national care service for the elderly needs to be set up to deal with this complex issue. At the moment it appears to be a ticking time bomb with a slow burning fuse.

Source: Economax tutor2u, April 2011

Question 13.1

Discuss the extent to which the government should intervene to regulate the care home market.

Question 13.2

Distinguish bulk-buying economies of scale from monopsony power.

Question 13.3

Explain why the following may have monopsony power:

(i) Amazon
(ii) NHS
(iii) British Sugar

The relationship between inputs and outputs in an economy can be shown using a production function. The quantity of output is said to be a function of inputs such as the quantity of labour (L), physical capital (machinery, buildings etc)(K), human capital (the accumulation of investment in people) (H) and the quantity of natural resources (N). This is often shown as Y = f(L,K,H,N) When these inputs are combined they produce, with the available technology, outputs. If inputs increase by 10% and outputs as a result also increase by 10% this is called constant returns to scale. If outputs had increased by 15% it is called increased returns to scale whereas only a 5% increase in outputs is decreased returns to scale. However, if technology improves then the economy can produce more output from a given combination of inputs as technology can benefit all of these inputs. Think how robots have improved labour productivity in car factories and how the mobile phone has helped workers who spend their time on the road visiting customers. Improved technology will thus increase the productivity of factors of production in an economy. The impact of technological change on an economy is to shift the production possibility frontier to the right (Figure 14.1) and is associated with dynamic efficiency which increases the choice, quality and performance of the goods and services available in the economy.

Figure 14.1

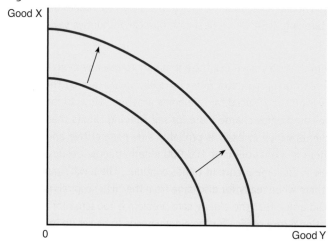

Economists often link dynamic efficiency with the pace of invention and innovation in a market. The difference between invention and innovation will be examined below. Technological change which comes from more advanced technological knowledge is the main reason for the growth in living standards over the last one hundred years. The telephone, the internal combustion engine, the jet engine, the computer and the internet have all increased the ability of firms to produce goods and services. Technological change comes from research by individuals, universities and firms and the government has a role in encouraging the advancement of knowledge. Grants, tax relief and the legal protection of new ideas through the patent system are used by the government to spur innovation.

Invention and innovation

Very often invention and innovation are used interchangeably but they are quite different despite being linked to the advancement of technology. Invention is about discovering a new product, or finding new ways of making products. It is an act of intellectual creativity but on its own has no economic significance. Innovation involves bringing this new idea to the market; that is turning an invention into a product that will deliver sales and profit. There are many inventions that are never developed commercially sometimes because there is not a large enough market to make a profit from it. In other words it cannot be 'scaled up'. Even when a new idea is commercially developed it can take several years before an invention earns any money for the inventor. Funds are needed to protect the idea and complying with industry design regulations is complex requiring skill and patience. A good example of the gap from invention to innovation is that of a portable incubator for premature babies. This was invented by James Roberts, a Loughborough University student, two years ago. It runs for 24 hours from a car battery and costs a 30th of a normal incubator. This invention could have a massive impact on the reduction of infant mortality in developing countries where there is often no mains electricity. However, it will be at least three more years before it is ready for the market. Put simply from laboratory to mass production is time consuming, costly and fraught with risk.

There are two types of innovation process and product. **Process innovation** occurs when a new production technique is applied to an existing product. For example the making of new cars has changed enormously as robots and computer aided manufacture have replaced assembly lines dominated by labour intensive production methods based on the division of labour. **Product innovation** occurs when firms create a new product or improve an existing product. The mobile phone was a new product thirty years ago but has been improved significantly over the years. The Mini car was introduced in 1959 but almost 60 years later is still on the market with a number of innovations now included in the car. Process innovation should lead to increases in productivity and lower costs per unit while product innovation if successful will increase sales and profits. These concepts have a link to dynamic efficiency in Unit 12.

A process innovation in an industry often affects and benefits all the firms in that industry whatever their size. Bar coding on groceries has benefitted both small and large supermarkets and has reduced their costs. The diagram below (Figure 14.2) shows the downward shift in the long run average cost curve with costs falling for all firms in that industry even those with a low level of output.

Figure 14.2

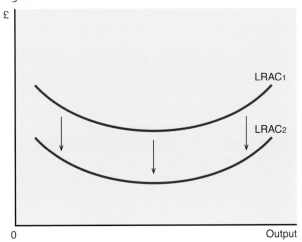

It was **Joseph Schumpeter** who introduced innovation into economic analysis through the term **creative destruction** which is defined as 'the incessant product and process innovation mechanism by which new production units replace outdated ones'. Over the long run, the process of creative destruction accounts for over 50 per cent of productivity growth. Creative destruction can be seen today as CDs are increasingly replaced by MP3 players and digital music downloads. DVDs which themselves replaced video cassettes may go the same way as films are watched instead through internet streaming.

Schumpeter describes the act of new innovations replacing old innovations as "creative destruction". This process is driven by the inevitable copying of new innovations, which causes profit margins to become low and creates a new incentive to seek out new innovations. This could be applied to the pharmaceutical industry where companies such as GSK and Pfizer invent and innovate new drugs which make them significant profits while still covered by patent protection. However, once the patent has expired generic drug producers enter the market and sell these drugs very cheaply which incentivises the pharmaceutical industry to invent new drugs to maintain their profits. Schumpeter would argue that creative destruction

will lead to some firms closing causing unemployment in the short term. However for technology to advance and living standards to rise this is necessary in the long term. The closure of bookshops affected by Amazon and also the demise of music stores selling CDs as a result of the growth of downloading are examples of this.

The effects of technological change

Over the years technological change has had a significant impact on production. Take land for example; modern fertilisers, drainage systems and farm equipment have significantly improved crop yields. The application of technology has also improved output per worker in arable farming – fewer workers are needed but yields are higher. In newspaper production the printing of a daily newspaper changed massively in the 1980s away from linotype or hot metal machines to computer typesetting. Traditional skills and working practices in the newspaper industry that had lasted for decades changed for ever.

Television sets were extremely expensive when they were first introduced. An early colour television bought in the late 1960s would cost over £300 – a huge amount relative to wages at the time. By 2015 a 32 inch colour television could be bought for just over £100 and it would have a better picture than 50 years ago! Comparisons of this kind are always difficult when some people currently pay over £2,000 for a top of the range television but today's basic television set is cheaper, more reliable and with a better quality picture thanks to the application of product and process innovation. The application of new technology can thus bring down costs and increase the price and non-price competitiveness of goods and services. The low price of tickets on the budget airlines is partly explained by their ability to apply new technology to keep costs down. The emergence of Ryanair and easyJet in the 1990s coincided with the growth of the internet. Passengers could book online, check-in online and print their boarding passes online – saving the airlines huge amounts of money. Thanks to the internet the airlines' ability to vary the cost of flights to passengers according to their demand in order to increase 'load factors' (seat occupancy levels) is very useful as a means of increasing revenue.

New technology has also created many new products – the kindle, the tablet, the sat nav – and also affected other more traditional markets. Many thought that the kindle would lead to the demise of the traditional book. However, this has proved not to be the case and by 2015 sales of new kindles had stagnated, everyone who wanted one had one and the market was saturated with many people still reading books in hard copy. The sat nav has not led to the end of the road atlas but the sat nav is winning. In 2009 1.37m road atlases and maps were sold, according to Nielsen BookScan, which compiles *The Sunday Times* bestsellers list. That dropped to 751,154 in 2013. Unofficially 2014 was expected to be the first year in which the majority of drivers use sat navs rather than road atlases. As mentioned early music downloads have seen the decline of the CD although the predecessor of CDs, vinyl records, has seen a significant renaissance in recent years.

It is also worth noting that online shopping and ecommerce generally has had significant effects. A very small firm once it has set up a website can sell its products nationally or even globally whereas thirty years ago it could never hope to reach much more than a local market. The internet has also allowed firms to exploit the Long Tail as it is known in marketing. Traditionally in most consumer markets 80% of the sales are generated from the best-selling 20% of the products sold. Shops and distributors tended to stock only those popular products but online buying means that a significant number of sales can be generated from the other less popular products – the tail. The internet allows booksellers such as Amazon to sell rather obscure niche market books such as A History of London's gasworks for example. The same goes for films and music where little known movies or records will be downloadable from Netflix or iTunes. Taken as a whole the 'tail' products can generate significant revenues for online sellers.

Technological change and market structure

How do advances in technology affect market structure? In some cases developments in technology have helped to make a market more contestable and brought about increased levels of competition. The successful entry of budget airlines into the air passenger travel market in Europe can be partly explained by these airlines using the internet to their advantage. Ryanair and easyJet by using the internet to facilitate flexible pricing (yield management), on line booking and check in as well as the printing of boarding cards helped produce a low cost business model which the more traditional airlines such as British Airways have had to catch up with. Other budget airlines have seen significant growth in their market share over the last twenty years although market size has increased at the same time.

The growth of Amazon also owed its success to the internet with people able to buy books at lower prices than in traditional high street bookshops such as Waterstones. While Amazon's rise in popularity has led to the demise of many bookshops and their increased market dominance many bookshops such as Waterstones do still survive as people enjoy browsing. Amazon is now the UK's eighth largest retailer and has through its Kindle device 95% of eBook sales. Ironically Amazon Marketplace provides a useful web based outlet for the products of small firms.

In car manufacturing the product and process innovation that has occurred in the last 20 years has probably contributed to increased concentration in the industry globally. There are huge research and development costs involved in developing a new model for the mass car market. Meeting safety and environmental standards as well as developing new devices such as 'parking assist' used by Ford are extremely costly. Mass car production requires heavy investment in robotics which although improve productivity and quality are very expensive. The successful car makers these days such as Nissan, Toyota, Ford and VW are very large businesses and to apply new technology they need to have the financial resources available. Many years ago the British car industry had many relatively small car makers such as, Wolseley, Austin, Triumph, Rover etc. Over the years they became amalgamated first into British Leyland and later the Rover Group. However, even this company was small by global standards and was unable to survive and went out of business in 2005. Rather tellingly Rover Group was said by one analyst to be too small to be big and too big to be small. This meant that Rover was no longer large enough to have the resources to produce successful new mass market cars such as the Mini in the 1960s. Equally the company was too big to be a successful niche, luxury car producer although it could have gone in that direction if tough decisions had been taken earlier; these being closures and redundancies. Ironically Rover Group had been owned by BMW from 1994 to 2000 but even they, with significant investment, could not turn the company round and sold it to the Phoenix Venture Holdings in 2000. BMW did keep the Mini within their ownership though and applying product and process innovation completely re-engineered the car and with great success. There is now a booming car industry in Britain but it is all foreign owned apart from niche producers such as Morgan and Bristol.

If a market is contestable does this encourage or discourage research and development and the consequent application of new technology? Some would argue that if a market is contestable with a constant threat of entry then existing firms may spend more on investing in new technology to gain an advantage over potential entrants. On the other hand firms in a contestable market may only be making normal profits and not have the resources to invest in new technology. Where a market has high barriers to entry it could be argued that firms will invest heavily in new technology because any increase in profits that are made as a result of applying this technology will not attract new entrants and dilute the benefits of new products and processes. In addition industries where the market is not contestable firms are more likely to be earning abnormal profit and have the resources to develop new technology.

Question 14.1

To what extent is technological knowledge a public good?

Question 14.2

Investigate the economic potential of graphene.

http://www.bbc.co.uk/news

http://www.graphene.manchester.ac.uk/explore/the-story-of-graphene/

https://en.wikipedia.org/wiki/Graphene

Unit 15: **Privatisation and regulation**

Privatisation can take a number of forms:

1. Sale of state owned shares in companies. This is the type of privatisation with which the public has become most familiar in recent years.

2. Contracting out of services previously provided by the state, under the process known as compulsory competitive tendering. Examples include school cleaning; refuse collection and council owned leisure centres.

3. The selling of individual state assets such as council houses and government buildings.

4. Deregulation. UK bus services were deregulated in 1986. However, a 2014 report by the Institute for Public Policy Research argued that deregulation had not resulted in a competitive market. It found that 37% of weekly bus services outside London do not face any real competition and only 1% of weekly services actually had genuine competition over all or most of their routes. In addition between 1995 and 2013 bus fares outside London rose by 35% above inflation. The report calls for the creation of local transport authorities modelled on Transport for London which, with some success, implements the transport strategy and manages transport services across the city. Bus passenger journeys outside London have fallen by 32.5% since 1986, but within London they have risen by 99%.

When the Conservative government was elected in 1979 it was on a set of radical policies which included extensive privatisation. From 1979 onwards British Telecom, British Gas, British Steel, water supply, electricity distribution, British Airports and railways were just some industries and firms transferred to private ownership. Most privatisations created new PLCs with shareholders buying their stake from the government. These newly privatised firms were thus fully listed companies on the Stock Exchange.

The privatisation of the railways was always very controversial and Railtrack's debts of £3.3bn coupled with an urgent need to raise £2bn led to the government in October 2001 invoking the Railway Act, which put the company into administration. When Railtrack was a PLC there was allegedly a conflict between profit paid to shareholders and new investment. There was always the feeling that safety was compromised in attempting to reduce costs and raise profits. Subsequently **Network Rail** was created which was initially a not-for-profit company operated on a commercial basis funded by banks and bondholders.

One of the most significant privatisations in recent years is that of Royal Mail. By October 2015 the government had completed its sale of the company raising a total of £3.3bn from the privatisation with 12% of the shares owned by Royal Mail employees. The privatisation was opposed by the trade unions, especially the Communication Workers Union (CWU), who believed with some justification that the company had been sold off cheaply and that the privatisation put a centuries old service in jeopardy. When the remaining government stake was sold the CWU general secretary Dave Ward said: "The remaining government share in this profitable company should have been used to safeguard the public's voice in the Royal Mail and ensure the continuation of daily deliveries to every address in the country." It is important to note that the Post Office remains in the public sector. Now called Post Office Ltd this is the organisation that provides a wide range of products including postage stamps and banking to the public through its network of post office branches many of which have been relocated to retail outlets such as supermarkets and WH Smith.

The privatisation process in the UK has been complemented by the deregulation or liberalisation of markets in which state owned firms once operated. This involves the removal of barriers that have previously prevented the emergence of competition (the bus industry, financial services and more recently postal services are examples). Where privatisation has not been considered appropriate, as with the NHS, **internal markets** have been created to bring competition. The internal market (a purchaser-provider system) in the NHS was introduced over 25 years ago through the 1990 NHS and Community Care Act. The government gives the money for the NHS to organisations called Clinical Commissioning Groups (CCGs), to buy services from providers (like hospitals). CCGs are clinically led groups that include all of the GP group practices in a geographical area. The aim of this is to give GPs and other clinicians the power to influence commissioning decisions for their patients. The job of the CCG is to establish contracts with the hospital trusts that ensure high quality, cost effective services for the local population. The idea of having the buying power in the hands of the CCGs is that it will create an effective internal market leading to competition between providers such as the hospital trusts leading to a decrease in costs and an increase in quality.

The idea is that the NHS will become more efficient and deliver better care as a result of being split into a number of purchasers who acquire care from a range of competing providers, rather than operating centrally although NHS England oversees the organisation which is the fifth biggest employer in the world with 1.7m employees. Creating a market of this kind is designed to produce the benefits of a normal competitive market. The 2012 Health and Social Care Act formalised into law further developments in the internal market that had occurred since 1990.

In the four years from 2012 the NHS needed to make efficiency savings of £20 billion which is 4 per cent per year to bridge the gap between a virtual freeze in real-terms funding, and rising demand. Its chances of doing this will depend on whether hospitals can improve productivity and efficiency. With an ageing population and increasing costs of drugs and medical equipment demand on the NHS will surge over the next 20 years and the new reforms are designed to reduce the cost base of the organisation. It is a matter of debate as to whether these reforms form the basis of the partial privatisation of the NHS. The NHS already contracts out health services to the private sector to the value of £20bn.

The aims of privatisation

1. **Improving efficiency.** In particular, the former nationalised industries were accused of X-inefficiency. The profit goal, which would now be pursued due to accountability to shareholders, would ensure a drive to eliminate this.

2. **Improving the quality and range of services.** The profit goal, combined with the 'discipline of the market', would lead to the attainment of this target: A high quality, wide-range, of services would be required in order to win custom.

3. **Lower prices.** These would result from competition.

4. **Widening of share ownership.** If more of the labour force become shareholders, it is likely that they will not view the owners of the companies for which they work as capitalists who appropriate the fruits of the labour of the workers. This is because as shareholders they too would be capitalists.

5. **Revenue raising.** The sale of state owned assets and shares deliver a one-off boost to government revenue and therefore a reduction in public sector borrowing.

6. **The creation of companies who, disciplined by the market, would become strong enough to be world leaders, competing on an international scale** which has happened with British Gas, National Grid and British Telecom.

It is important to note that the achievement of some of these goals is heavily dependent on the measures, complementary to privatisation, to introduce competition. *Ceteris paribus*, the privatisation of a state monopoly creates a private monopoly and exposes the economy to the high prices and inefficient resource allocation that this is likely to entail. However, with the introduction of competition, we have good reason to expect a greater degree of allocative and technical efficiency, together with lower prices. It is partly for this reason that regulatory bodies have been set up to oversee the privatised industries. The aim is to protect the consumer from the potential abuse of monopoly power, and, indeed, from any undesirable side effects of competition. Regulation is particularly important in the water industry where domestic consumers face a regional monopoly.

Has privatisation been successful?

Between 1979 and 1997, when most of the privatisations took place, the proceeds from privatisation were some £90 billion. Firms which were loss making under public ownership began to make a profit. A study of 33 privatised enterprises found that, prior to privatisation, they absorbed £500 million of public funds annually and £1 billion in loan finance. Although the rail network continues to receive financial support, albeit dwindling, from the Treasury the privatised firms are no longer the burden they were in the 1970s. The real prices (prices adjusted for inflation) of gas and electricity fell in the 1990s as competition drove down

energy bills and much the same occurred in telecommunications. However, there has long been a suspicion that the big six energy companies in the UK are very quick to raise their gas charges to customers when the wholesale gas price rises but very slow to cut charges when the wholesale price falls. The former Energy Secretary Chris Huhne said, when in office, he had concerns that prices to customers had gone "up like a rocket and down like a feather" in response to changes in wholesale prices. Some analysts believed that high UK energy prices were due to **tacit collusion** among the big six suppliers. It has often been asserted that many consumers have failed to benefit from all the price competition in the telecoms and energy markets because they are either unaware that the company they are using is not the cheapest or they cannot be bothered to switch suppliers; the term **customer inertia** is used by economists to describe this phenomenon.

Despite web sites such as www.simplyswitch.com many domestic consumers overpay on their energy bills. Those who have a dual fuel arrangement with their suppler and who pay by direct debit allegedly pay less per unit of energy than those who have separate suppliers or who use pre-payment meters. This could be an example of price discrimination which penalises those on low incomes. Energy suppliers may well point to the lower costs of administering dual fuel accounts made monthly by direct debit. From 1990 to 2011 the average energy bill rose from £530 to £1140, a rise of 115%.

Figure 15.1

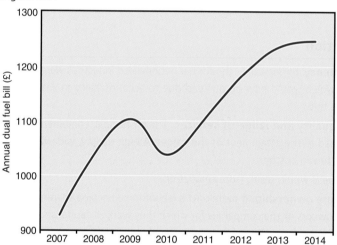

In recent years the rising price of energy can be seen in Figure 15.1 above which arguably could be linked to tacit collusion. This issue and the seemingly rather opaque and dysfunctional energy market led to the regulator Ofgem referring the energy market to the Competition and Markets Authority which has more extensive powers to address any long-term structural barriers to competition. The Competition and Markets Authority found that between 2009 and 2013, British Gas, E.On, Npower, EDF Energy, Scottish Power and SSE collectively charged households £1.2bn a year more than they would have in a competitive market. They also found dual fuel customers could save £160 a year on average by switching supplier. It is worth noting that the breakdown of a dual fuel bill shown below makes it quite difficult to assess the extent to which the Big Six energy suppliers have been guilty of price fixing.

Breakdown of an annual dual fuel bill (Nov 2014-Oct 2015)

What makes up the bill?	Cost	Proportion of bill
Wholesale costs	£588	44%
Network costs excl. green costs	£305	23%
Green costs (inc. ROCs, ECO, feed-in-tariffs, Government rebates)	£91	7%
Suppliers' operating costs	£175	13%
VAT (tax)	£63	5%
Pre-tax profit margin	£105	8%
Total	**£1,327**	**100%**

Source: Ofgem

Average annual water bills have risen significantly in real terms since privatisation in 1989 and the price limits set for 2005-2010 meant that the average household customer paid about £46 more in real terms by 2009-2010 than in 2004-05, an increase of around 18%.

In the past water companies were allowed real terms price increases to cover the cost of massive water infrastructure improvements. This was a formula called RPI+K where K is the allowance for spending on increased investment by the company. However, the 2015-2020 water price regime set by the water regulator Ofwat has ruled that household water bills in England and Wales will fall by an average of 5% – not including RPI inflation – by 2020. RPI is usually higher than CPI inflation, and was around 1% in 2015. Thames Water has been told it will have to cut charges by 5% in real terms and United Utilities by 3%. This means that if RPI inflation was 3% Thames Water bills would fall by 2% in nominal terms but by 5% in real terms. This is called RPI−X where X is the 5% set by the regulator.

Changes in water bills 2015 to 2019

Company	Average bill by 2019, before RPI	Average change, before RPI
Anglian	£390	-10%
Dwr Cymru	£416	-5%
Northumbrian (inc. Essex and Suffolk)	£382	-1%
Severn Trent	£316	-5%
Southern	£403	-8%
South West	£506	-7%
Thames	£353	-5%
United Utilities	£398	-3%
Wessex	£442	-9%
Yorkshire	£361	-3%

Given these figures it would seem to be very hard to argue against privatisation. However, the collapse of Railtrack and the fact that rail fares have risen in real terms since 1997 indicate that rail privatisation has not been a great success. In addition the standard of service on routes worsened post-privatisation for several years. Although there was a rise in passenger miles travelled after privatisation the rail service was hampered by under-investment, regulatory confusion and an over complex fares structure. However, of late there have been improvements to both rolling stock and track infrastructure as investment has begun to pay off and increasingly trains are arriving on time. There has been substantial investment via the taxpayer in the rail infrastructure, but in recent years financial support to the rail sector has fallen. Pressure on the rail network will continue with the number of rail journeys in Britain at their highest since 1947.

Figure 15.2

Source: ONS   Rail fares % change based on CPI, regarded as best statistical measure by ONS

Rail fares in the UK are controlled by the Department of Transport. Some fares such as season tickets and day returns are regulated and at present these are limited to increases equal to RPI inflation thus in real terms they are unchanged year on year. However a large number of rail fares are not regulated and the train operating companies are able to make their own decisions on charging. Rail remains an expensive way to travel unless passengers book in advance and many trade unions and politicians would like to see railways back in public ownership. Britain is one of the most expensive places in Europe to travel by train. The Campaign for Better Transport said the cost of a Milton Keynes to London season ticket had risen by 23.5% – or £930 – since January 2010. The price of a 2015 season ticket was £4,888. With government financial support to the railways falling and new investment still needed there is little prospect of Britain's railways getting cheaper in the near future (see Figure 15.2). Many analysts see the railways as a botched privatisation by separating the

Britain is one of the most expensive places in Europe to travel by train.

operation of the track and signals (Network Rail) from the train operating companies such as Virgin and First Great Western as well as creating a myriad of other companies relating to the leasing of rolling stock and maintenance. Rail is seen by many economists and railway engineers alike as a **natural monopoly**.

More recently the part privatisation of National Air Traffic (NATS) was heavily criticised by the airline industry and trade unions. Privatisation led to huge job losses in the coal, steel and telephone sectors. In addition the desire for wide shareholder ownership among the population has not been achieved to any significant degree. In addition contracting out of public sector services such as hospital cleaning and court security has often led to a decline in quality.

2015-16 has been a bumper year for asset sales by the government as Figure 15.3 shows. The Conservative government raised £31 billion in 2015-16 by selling off publicly owned assets, the most ever raised from privatisation in a single year even when adjusted for inflation. Further privatisations cannot be ruled out in the years ahead (see Question 15.3).

Figure 15.3: Real value of corporate and financial asset sales from 1977-78 to 2015-16

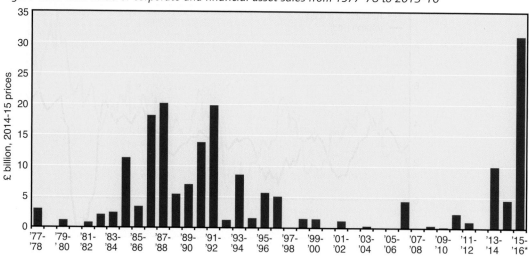

Source: Business Insider UK   *Planned

The activities of regulatory bodies

The main functions of regulatory agencies such as Ofwat (water industry) and Ofcom (telecommunications and postal services) and Ofgem (energy) are to control prices in the privatised utility markets, to prevent consumer exploitation and, where necessary, to take account of the existence of externalities. Judging which price level will deliver an efficient resource allocation is thus a difficulty that the regulators face.

Regulators attempt to create the constraints and stimuli which companies experience in a competitive market environment. They thus simulate the effects of competition by price caps and quality standards. Price caps are usually based on a satisfactory rate of profit on the value of assets employed. Performance indicators such as the number of trains that are late or water leakages assess quality standards. The table below relates to the performance of Thameslink.

Passenger satisfaction

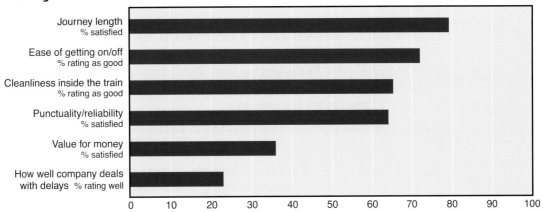

Regulators attempt to encourage competition by easing the entry of new products and preventing privatised firms erecting or maintaining barriers to entry. The regulator should thus promote effective competition and remove market distortions helping to make markets more contestable. Legislation now allows regulators to fine companies for breaches of licence conditions. Regulators don't have as much investigative power as the Competition and Markets Authority (CMA) and can refer firms to the CMA for a detailed investigation as occurred with the energy sector in 2014.

Types of regulation

1. RPI-X

RPI-X means that permitted price increases are determined by the percentage rise in the retail price index (RPI) minus an amount X, where X is the reduction in price required for the industry as a result of expected improvements in efficiency. So for telecoms, between 1997 and 2002 the price formula was RPI – 4.5 per cent (the formula only applied to some customers). This meant that if inflation was 8 per cent, BT would be allowed to raise its prices by only 8% – 4.5% = 3.5%. If inflation was 3 per cent, BT would have to put its price down by 1.5% i.e. 3% – 4.5% = –1.5%. In 2009 regulated rail fares rose by over 6% as the train operators were able to use the July 2008 RPI inflation rate of 5.2% as the basis of their fares structure. These price rises were unpopular with rail users faced with the recession and the credit crunch. Train operators said at the time that the fare increases were necessary to improve the standard of service and these companies felt that if the RPI fell to the extent that retail inflation was negative (deflation) – a possibility during a recession – then fares would have to be cut.

In October 2010 it was announced that regulated rail fares would rise by RPI+3% for three years from January 2012. An RPI + X price regime is associated with a fall in government subsidy as was the case with passenger rail services in the UK. However, the Government later announced a reversion back to RPI+1% for 2013 and 2014, and then changed the regime again limiting fare rises to just RPI for 2014 and 2015. Subsequent to their election victory the Conservative government announced that regulated rail fares in England would rise by no more than RPI inflation for this parliament which means until 2020. For passengers there is anger that rail fares in Britain are much higher than those in mainland Europe and that it costs up to 30% more to run the railway in Britain than in countries such as Germany and Switzerland.

The problem for the RPI-X system is setting the figure for X. The company needs to provide accurate information about its costs to the regulator but will it? If the regulator sets X too high then the company will have insufficient funds to invest and the standard of service will fall leading to dynamic inefficiency. If X is set too low then excessive profits will be earned. There is also the problem of how long the X factor should be set for. If it's too long then changes in market conditions cannot be taken into account; too short and there is not enough of a time scale for companies to plan ahead with long term investments.

On the other hand RPI-X regulation does give firms the opportunity to plan investment programmes and estimate with some accuracy their revenue streams. For example National Grid which is responsible for the transportation and transmission of gas and electricity was subject to the RPI-X regulation for around 20 years. The regulator Ofgem used price controls to incentivise National Grid to achieve efficiency savings, although a new system of regulation, RIIO (Revenue, Incentives, Innovation, Outputs), is about to be introduced (see Question 15.4).

Water companies in the UK are regional monopolies, but they were in the past allowed by their regulator Ofwat to increase real prices using a K factor formula. The K factor is the annual rate by which each licensed water company could increase its charges annually on top of inflation. The K factors were set by Ofwat at a price review, for the next five years. Water companies were allowed to increase their real prices because of the substantial investment required in new infrastructure and the need to meet environmental standards laid down by the European Union.

The following table illustrates what happened to average household water bills in the area covered by Southern Water under their business plan for the regulatory period 2010-2015.

Year	2010/11	2011/12	2012/13	2013/14	2014/15	
	5.3%	3.2%	3.2%	3.0%	0.0%	Average = **2.9%**

Ofwat limited the annual price increase, or K factor, for each water company to reflect what it needed to charge to finance the provision of services to customers i.e. capital investment. The K factor told the water company the percentage by which, in real terms it must increase – or must decrease prices – in each of the five years covered by the price review. Ofwat checked that the increases did not on average exceed inflation plus the K factor (K can be negative). Another form of price regulation is RPI + Y which involves the regulator making an allowance for a rise in costs given as Y which are out of the control of the firms in that sector. These costs are thus allowed to be passed on to consumers by the regulator.

Price capping, particularly RPI – X, is seen as an appropriate way to control firms with significant monopoly power who may be natural monopolies. When RPI – X is used the cut in real price levels is good for households and business users affecting in turn consumer surplus and cost levels and also helping to control inflation. When firms have their prices capped it should encourage them to reduce their costs and increase productivity. On the other hand price caps can lead to job losses and the price controls set by regulators distort the workings of the price mechanism. Price caps also rely on the regulators collecting all the relevant market information and getting their decision right, for that they need expertise as well as resources.

2. Licencing/Franchising

Rail services and the National Lottery are good examples of granting licences or franchises to firms and giving them significant monopoly power. Following the abolition of the Strategic Rail Authority in 2005 the Department of Transport became responsible for the issue of franchises to the Train Operating Companies. There has been much controversy in the rail industry regarding the length of franchises. In the early days after rail privatisation franchises ran for 15 years but they can be less than half that. Short franchises (some have been less than six years) give the train operators little time to plan investment effectively and mean that they are reliant on the train leasing companies. Longer franchises would encourage operators to invest in rolling stock which lasts 20 years or more.

The Brown Review on Rail Franchising (2013) said that the length of a rail franchise should be determined by the circumstances and size of each individual franchise. His report felt that a franchise should "usually consist of a 7 to 10 year initial term with pre-contracted continuation, subject to agreed franchise criteria being met, for further terms of 3 to 5 years giving eventual terms of up to 15 years, but with intermediate break points." The report felt that shorter or longer franchises are sometimes appropriate, but a franchise term should not be less than 5 years. Indeed government policy reflects this as they expect franchises to run for between 7-10 years but the particular circumstances of each franchise might mean it is appropriate for a longer or shorter contract. A selection of current franchises and their length are shown below:

Chiltern Railways (Arriva) – 2002-2021
Cross Country Trains (Arriva) – 2007-2016
East Coast Trains (Inter City Railways) – 2015-2023
Scot Rail (Abellio) – 2015-2025
South West Trains (Stagecoach) – 2007-2017

Larger franchises are supported by the rail sector because it gives train operators more time to invest in and profit from new rolling stock, although operators face big financial penalties if they don't complete a franchise because they are finding it unprofitable. In 2005 GNER (National Express) won the franchise for the East Coast Mainline but in 2009 defaulted on the terms of its franchise and the line was taken into public ownership by the government under a department called Directly Operated Railway.

The National Lottery is a good example of granting a licence to a firm, giving it significant monopoly power.

The East Coast franchise was successfully re-let in 2015 to Inter City Railways Limited, a consortium of Stagecoach Group (90%), and Virgin Trains (10%). The company is now trading under the name of Virgin Trains East Coast.

The National Lottery Commission, part of the Gambling Commission, the regulator, announced in 2007 that Camelot was to be appointed as the operator to run The National Lottery from 2009-2019. The National Lottery Commission has agreed to extend the company's licence, which was due to expire in 2019, by another four years. As part of the agreement, the company said it would set up 8,000 new outlets in areas where it had identified 'untapped demand' for lottery tickets. Camelot has operated the National Lottery since its inception in 1994. The licence to run the lottery carries with it numerous conditions and Camelot must stay within its licence or risk fines or other punishment. However, the firm does have a legalised monopoly similar to the train operating companies such as First Great Western and Virgin Trains. If the length of the franchise is set correctly for the industry licensing brings together the benefits of competition (in the bidding process) with those of a natural monopoly.

3. Rate of return regulation

This form of regulation includes the regulator setting what it thinks is a 'normal' rate of return on the capital employed in the business. This rate of return is set higher than the interest paid to acquire the capital. The government then taxes at 100% any profit made above this 'normal' rate. The problem for this form of regulation is that firms have no incentive to be efficient beyond a certain level. If they work very hard to improve efficiency and raise their profits as a consequence they will find these extra profits taxed away as a result of all their efforts! Thus higher investment and attempts to raise productivity are not incentivised.

Rate of return regulation also has the problem that it encourages firms to overvalue their assets. If they are allowed to make a 10% return on their assets then it would be in their financial interests to falsely value them at £100m than at the correct figure of say £75m. A 10% return on £100m is £10m and far better than £7.5m.

4. Yardstick competition

Sometimes the regulator uses the performance of different firms in the industry to set price and customer service standards. It is used when the firms are regionally separate and there may be no direct competition, such as exists with the UK water authorities. The best performing firms thus set the standard and are used as a yardstick for the rest of the industry when a price regime is formulated. In theory it is possible for the regulator to use yardstick competition to maximise efficiency and eliminate abnormal profits when cost changes across firms are analysed. However, the precise way in which comparative cost information is used in price reviews by regulators such as Ofwat is often unclear and sometimes comparisons appear to be subjective. Geographical, climatic and geological differences between the water regions make this difficult.

Judging the effectiveness of regulation

These questions could be asked when assessing the success of a regulator.

1. What has been the effect of regulation on:
   - real prices to customers?
   - levels of competition in the industry?
   - employment and productivity levels in the industry?
   - the quality of service?
   - investment levels in the industry?

2. How far has the regulator been able to adapt to changes in market conditions and technology? i.e. from monitoring the performance of a single firm towards assessing the performance of a competitive market as a whole.

3. To what extent will the regulator be able to bring about market conditions, which reduce its role to relatively minor issues? The regulator initially acts in place of competition in a monopolistic market; will it be able to make itself redundant in time?

4. How far has the regulator been able to make the market more contestable?

5. How effective has the regulator been at discovering and dealing with abuses of dominant positions in a market such as predatory pricing and market sharing?

How successful has regulation been in the UK?

The regulator is there to encourage competition in an industry that may have been privatised as a monopoly. If there is no competition, possibly because the industry is a natural monopoly then the regulator's duty is to make the firm act as though they were operating in a competitive market. Once there is competition in the market the regulator has to consider the prices charged by firms and the quality of service they provide. Regulators will also seek to reduce barriers to entry to the market, such as the pressure placed on BT in recent years by Ofcom to open up the 'local loop' in its line infrastructure to other telecoms firms so that they can provide telephone and internet services. This led to the creation of a separate company within BT called Openreach.

The UK regulators were given industry structures to work with, post privatisation, some were good others not so good. The initial fall in real prices in gas, electricity and telecoms was encouraging but the consumer has paid for the massive investment needed in the water infrastructure through higher water bills. In time increased competition will replace many aspects of regulation, but many markets will remain dominated by a few large firms and the electricity and gas infrastructure will remain a natural monopoly, as will water quite probably. In addition even when a market is competitive firms may fail to take into account environmental or social objectives.

The RPI-X formula can potentially lead to huge improvements in efficiency but has the regulator always been dealing with accurate information when setting price controls? How easy is it to set the value of X? However, regulators are independent and do not have to answer to the government or the firms involved. With their specialist knowledge it can be argued that they are the best people to decide whether the firms in an industry are acting in the public interest. Regulators have a long term future in these markets despite the increase in competition. There may appear to be a competitive market but regulators may find that the market may not be working effectively, a view that many felt applied to the UK energy market in 2008 when it was investigated by Ofgem. Markets such as energy have arguably become dysfunctional with opaque and complex pricing and mis-selling of gas and electricity contracts. Regulators may not have sufficient powers to uncover many market abuses and have to refer their concerns to the Competition and Markets Authority.

Clearly some of the UK privatisations could have created better structures in their markets, this may be particularly true of rail and energy. Consequently the regulation of these industries has been difficult at times. In the rail sector it has been argued that the train leasing companies (ROSCOs) have made huge abnormal profits largely at the expense of passengers. ROSCOs lease the rolling stock to train operating companies such as Virgin and First Great Western. However, as markets evolve regulation has to adapt and in energy a new regulatory system for the National Grid has been created to respond to emissions targets and the closure of old coal fired power stations. Energy generation and transmission require significant investment over the coming years and regulation will need to reflect these changes.

One of the major problems facing regulators is dealing with information failure. Information failure exists when one participant in the buying or selling process knows more about the product or service than the other participant. This is called asymmetric information when ideally it should be symmetric i.e. balanced. The mis-selling of pensions, energy contracts and Payment Protection Insurance (PPI) are recent examples of this. PPI was often sold to people who didn't need it or wouldn't benefit from it. Over-complex pricing for railway tickets and energy has shown up further information problems where people do not have perfect knowledge of what they trying to buy.

Regulation of the financial sector

The creation of the **Financial Policy Committee** (**FPC**), the **Prudential Regulation Authority** (**PRA**) and the **Financial Conduct Authority** (**FCA**) stem from the financial crisis of 2008-09, the so called 'credit crunch'. The crisis showed very clearly the dangers of poor regulation in banking and financial markets when there are asset bubbles, excessive levels of debt and dangerous risk taking by lenders and borrowers. Within banking and the financial markets it was agreements such as credit default swaps and sub prime mortgages which caused major concern because the the lack of transparency in these large markets became a concern to regulators as they posed a major risk to the whole financial system. The Financial Services Authority (FSA) was responsible for the regulation of the financial services industry

It has been argued that the train leasing companies have made huge profits largely at the expense of passengers.

in the United Kingdom between 2001 and 2013 and was blamed in part for the financial crisis. The government as a result completely reformed the regulatory regime in the banking and financial services sector.

The Financial Services Act 2012 gave the FPC overall responsibility for financial regulation by identifying, monitoring and addressing risks to the financial system as a whole; thus enhancing the system's resilience. The FPC's actions are designed to reduce uncertainty and boost confidence in the financial markets. The FPC has a secondary role of being charged with supporting the government's objectives of growth and employment and is part of the Bank of England.

Specifically the FPC can recommend a given course of action to any bank for example to reduce risk in the financial system. Alternatively it can give formal directions to the PRA and the FCA. For example the PRA which supervises the safety and soundness of firms in the financial sector by looking at levels of debt, credit growth, liquidity etc. could be directed to adjust the capital requirements of banks. This is the minimum level of capital they can hold in relation to loans. The FCA's role is to protect consumers of financial services from sharp practices such as the mis-selling of financial products as was seen recently with Payment Protection Insurance (PPI). The FCA recently produced the Mortgage Market Review which changed the way in which applications for mortgages are assessed. The regulatory framework in place during the housing boom years before the financial crisis had proved to be ineffective in reducing high-risk lending and borrowing. The Mortgage Market Review reforms were aimed at ensuring the continued access to mortgages for the great majority of customers who can afford it, while preventing a return to the poor practices where mortgages were granted without proper assessment of whether the borrowers would find the financial burden of a mortgage affordable over the long term.

One of the lessons of the credit crunch was that even when individual firms in the financial sector may appear sound when their activities are aggregated they pose major risks to the stability of the financial system. The regulatory framework which has now been introduced is designed to make the financial sector in the UK more robust while allowing it to continue to be a major employer and contributor to both GDP and the balance of payments.

Regulatory capture

Regulatory bodies are often accused of being too soft on the businesses that they regulate, which are still making huge profits. The issue of regulatory capture (where the regulator starts to serve the interests of the monopolists rather than limit their power) has often been raised. While there is little evidence to support the claim that this is happening, it remains likely that firms are able to influence regulators to some degree. Regulatory capture was possibly a reason why the electricity industry was able to enjoy a very lax regulatory regime from Offer (the then electricity regulator) in the mid-1990's. In 1998 Peter Davis, the head of OFLOT the then lottery regulator, resigned after it emerged that he accepted free flights from GTech, the parent company of Camelot, who run the UK's lottery. However, some regulators have taken a strong independent view and Tom Winsor in charge of the Office of Rail Regulation until 2004 was forthright in his criticism of government policy towards the railways in the UK, and had a stormy relationship with Railtrack (prior to it becoming Network Rail). There have also been accusations of weak or ineffective regulation by the Civil Aviation Authority (CAA) with regard to British airports (mainly BAA) and also prior to the financial crisis by the Financial Services Authority (FSA) in the banking sector. Whether these two examples amount to regulatory capture is more debatable. The key issue is the ability of the regulator to gain all the information they need from the firms and to act on it effectively in the interests of all stakeholders (customers, investors, and the firms themselves). Regulators often lack the resources, skills and powers to obtain all the relevant information they need from firms when trying to decide what action to take. Regulators also have fewer investigative powers than the Competition and Markets Authority.

Question 15.1

(a) Using examples explain what is meant by a natural monopoly.

(b) How could a natural monopoly be regulated?

Question 15.2

Evaluate the UK experience of RPI-X regulation.

Question 15.3

Which organisations are future candidates for privatisation up to 2020?

Question 15.4

Because price control mechanisms restrict revenues, not profits, they encourage efficiencies within our regulated businesses. Savings that are made can be retained for the remainder of the price control period, but the higher level of efficiency that led to these savings is then used to inform a new baseline level for the next price control period.

Price control regulation is designed to ensure that, as a monopoly, we charge reasonable prices, and to provide us with a future level of revenue sufficient to enable us to meet our statutory duties and licence obligations. It also provides financial incentives to manage and operate our networks in an economic, efficient and coordinated manner in accordance with our legal and licence obligations, offer good quality of service to network users and invest in our networks in a timely and efficient manner to help ensure long-term security of supply is maintained.

During each price control review period, the amount of money that can be earned by our regulated businesses is restricted by what is referred to as an RPI-X price control, which is normally reviewed every five years by Ofgem. The RPI-X allowance is based upon Ofgem's estimates of efficient operating expenditure, capital expenditure and asset replacement, together with an allowance for depreciation and an allowed rate of return on capital invested in our businesses. This is summarised in the diagram below, representing a building block model of the price control.

Building blocks

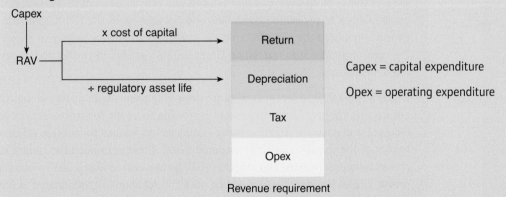

The inputs of the building block model are used, together with the **regulatory asset base value** (RAV) to calculate the allowed revenue. The RAV, which represents the value ascribed by Ofgem to the capital employed in our regulated businesses, is adjusted to reflect asset additions, removals, depreciation and the rate of inflation.

The RPI-X price control takes the retail price index as its benchmark and subtracts X, an efficiency factor, from it. For example, at a time when annual inflation was 3%, a value for X of 2% would allow our regulatory businesses to raise prices by no more than 1%. Price controls also include incentive mechanisms to encourage us to improve our performance in particular areas.

(Continued overleaf)

The price control provides our regulated businesses with a level of revenue that is sufficient to finance the businesses if they are efficiently run. The revenue allowance is based on an estimate of the costs an efficient company would face in running its regulated businesses and includes operating expenditure, capital expenditure, financing costs including both debt and equity, and taxation.

Current price controls

The key elements of the current price controls for both gas and electricity transmission are that we are allowed to earn a 4.4% post-tax real return on our RAV, equivalent to a 5.05% vanilla return, with a £4.4 billion baseline five year capex allowance and a £1.2 billion five year controllable opex allowance.

In addition, we are subject to a number of incentives that can adjust our transmission network revenue. For electricity transmission, these include incentives for network reliability, sulphur hexafluoride losses, efficiency and balancing services. For gas transmission, our incentive schemes cover areas such as the cost of investment for additional capacity to facilitate new connections to the system.

The key elements of the current price controls for gas distribution are that we are allowed to earn a 4.3% post-tax real rate of return on our RAV, equivalent to a 4.94% vanilla return, with a £2.5 billion baseline five year capex allowance and a £1.6 billion five year controllable opex allowance.

	RAV	Return on equity
Electricity transmission	£8,388m	13.6%
Gas transmission	£4,889m	15.8%
Gas distribution	£7,520m	12.1%
Total	£20,797m	13.6%

Ofgem's review of price controls: RPI–X@20

Since privatisation, the RPI-X mechanism has provided the industry with strong incentives to be more efficient. The level of opex costs has decreased over the years, transforming previously inefficient nationalised industries. However, over the past few years new challenges, such as Great Britain's transition to lower carbon emissions and the requirement to renew ageing networks, have caused Ofgem to review the continuing appropriateness of the RPI-X approach. In March 2008, Ofgem announced the RPI-X@20 review, which was a two year project to review the workings of the current approach to regulating Great Britain's energy networks and develop future policy recommendations.

Ofgem's RPI-X@20 review aims were to: drive improvements in quality of service and efficiency; ensure that the regulatory framework is flexible to adapt to structural changes in the energy industry; and enable efficient network companies to finance themselves efficiently. To allow the lessons of the review to be accommodated in full, Ofgem extended the current transmission price control from its scheduled end in March 2012 by one year to March 2013. Following the RPI-X@20 review, Ofgem has identified a modified price control approach, designated as RIIO, to deliver and meet the changing future needs of the energy market. RIIO stands for revenue, incentives, innovation and outputs.

Reproduced by the kind permission of National Grid PLC

Question: Investigate how RIIO will work in electricity transmission.

Unit 16: **Competition policy in the UK and the European Union**

Because of the link between competition and efficiency suggested by economic theory, competition authorities (in the UK the Competition and Markets Authority) are charged with preventing the abuse of monopoly power and guarding against restrictive practices. Restrictive, or anti-competitive, practices are those undertaken by a firm with a view to limiting competition in its markets. Predatory pricing is a prime example. The competition authority in the UK investigates activities, which prevent, restrict or distort competition.

In April 2014 the Competition and Markets Authority (CMA) replaced and took over the functions of the Office of Fair Trading (OFT) and the Competition Commission. The CMA investigates monopolies, mergers and cartels. In the case of monopolies it is concerned with abuse of dominance and how the incumbent firm makes it difficult for new firms to enter the market. Mergers that could lead to a substantial lessening of competition are likely to be subject to a detailed investigation. Any activity which restricts distorts or prevents competition, particularly cartels is likely to be investigated.

The new Competition and Markets Authority has stronger powers of investigation than its predecessors including the right to require individuals (i.e. directors) connected to a business under investigation for abuse of dominance or anti-competitive practices to answer questions. The new rules give the CMA stronger powers to order interim measures ordering firms to terminate certain commercial practices pending the outcome of an investigation. It will now also be easier for the CMA to bring criminal prosecutions for cartels. These new powers are laid down in the Enterprise and Regulatory Reform Act 2013 and supplement the provisions of the Competition Act 1998 and the Enterprise Act 2002.

An interesting new focus of the CMA compared to its predecessors is that it is increasingly prepared to investigate and rule on abuses of market dominance and anti-competitive practices which involve small firms. Schools have been warned about telling parents of pupils that they can only use one approved school uniform supplier. A group of estate agents in Surrey and Hampshire have been investigated for anti-competitive practices concerning the publication of their fees in local newspapers.

Mergers

When a possible merger would result in the newly merged company supplying at least 25% of the UK market and the UK turnover of the enterprise which is being acquired exceeds £70 million then there is potential threat to competition. If there is full investigation that concludes that there is a threat to competition the CMA will prevent the merger going ahead. In 2015 takeover of 99p stores by Poundland was investigated by the CMA for this reason but did not pass from a phase 1 initial examination to a phase 2 full investigation. This was because there would still be significant competition in that 'single price point market' from Poundworld and Poundstretcher as well as the supermarkets and other high street 'value' stores such as Wilkinsons. The merger was thus given clearance.

Monopolies

The CMA can also investigate monopolies which have large market shares and who could be abusing their dominant position. A firm with only a 25% market share could be investigated but it is usually at least 40%. Tesco has more than 25% of the grocery market but has substantial competition from Sainsbury and Asda. In recent years a major monopoly investigation involved British Airports Authority (BAA) which owned many major airports in the UK including all three in the London area. The CMA's predecessor the Competition Commission ordered BAA to sell a number of their airports including Stanstead, Gatwick and Edinburgh to other airport operators. This was designed to give their customers, the airlines, more choice in the provision of routes as well as boosting quality of service which BAA had been criticised for. More recently Openreach, the subsidiary of British Telecom (BT), which controls the local telephone network, has

been a target for a CMA investigation. Users of Openreach such as Sky and TalkTalk want BT to sell its network subsidiary as they believe it is unfair that it is owned by one of their competitors. They accuse BT of abusing their control of Openreach and want it to operate rather like the National Grid and Network Rail i.e. completely independently. A CMA investigation could order Openreach to be sold off as a completely separate company, but for the moment Openreach will remain part of BT.

Cartels

Cartels and other forms of collusion are nearly always seen as an anti-competitive practice because they distort, restrict or prevent competition. Firms can be fined up to 10% of turnover and directors prosecuted in the criminal courts which can result in imprisonment. **Price-fixing** is common in highly concentrated markets where the product is homogeneous. In recent years cement and energy are sectors in which the competition authorities have held investigations. It is often difficult to spot collusion when there is no record of meetings or exchange of commercially sensitive information. Very often the competition authorities have to rely on whistle blowing companies or employees which are involved in the cartel. The former usually receive reduced fines or immunity and employees can receive financial reward. What is often seen as price fixing is in fact tacit collusion or price leadership when firms appear to have acted as if they have an agreement but have had not been in contact with one another.

Examples of anti-competitive practice include:

1. **Predatory pricing** and **limit pricing**.
2. **Restriction of supply** to distributors.
3. **'Full-line forcing'.** The retailer is forced to stock the complete range of a manufacturer's products; otherwise he will not be supplied at all. This leaves little room for stocking competitors to the range.
4. Creation of **artificial barriers to entry**, through activities such as extremely high advertising expenditure or wide-ranging brand proliferation but this is rarely investigated.

Examples of other collusive restrictive practice include:

5. **Market sharing** and **collusive tendering**.
6. Agreements on types of goods to be produced or to co-ordinate investment.

Collusive behaviour involving more than 25% of the market is likely to be investigated although price fixing agreements, which have a dramatic effect at a local level, could also be eligible. Heating oil supply was a case in point some years ago.

Assessment of UK competition policy

The Competition Act (1998) and the **Enterprise Act (2002)** brought UK legislation more closely in line with European Union competition policy and legislation has shifted the focus to anti-competitive practices and their effects rather than on agreements and the size of a firm's market share. The competition authorities now place more emphasis on the contestability of markets rather than the assumption that structure determines conduct and performance. Mergers were not covered by the 1998 Act which means that there is no presumption that a merger is against the public interest, the Competition and Markets Authority (CMA) has to prove that there is a threat to competition. Most mergers are not referred to the CMA and there is plenty of evidence that many are not in the public interest nor in the interests of the merging firms.

Some mergers may not be in the public interest and be a genuine threat to competition but nevertheless go ahead possibly where the national interest is a priority. A good example comes from the financial crisis in 2008 when Lloyds TSB took over the struggling HBOS. This huge banking merger which gave Lloyds a massive share of retail banking was brokered by the Chancellor of the Exchequer Alistair Darling as part of his strategy to support a beleaguered banking sector. There is little doubt that this merger would never have been approved by the competition authorities in more stable economic conditions. Retail banking remains very highly concentrated in the UK despite the emergence of 'challenger banks' such as Metro Bank and the demerger of the TSB from Lloyds.

The Competition and Markets Authority has only been in existence for two years and it is too early to assess its effectiveness, but with additional powers contained in the Enterprise and Regulatory Reform Act it has the potential to ensure that markets remain genuinely competitive and abuse of dominance is identified and ceased. One of the major complaints levelled at its predecessors, the OFT and the Competition Commission, was the length of time it took to carry out a full investigation and make recommendations. Reform measures introduced by the Act speed up administrative procedures with powers to impose interim measures prior to full publication of a report.

Competition Appeal Tribunal

The Competition Appeal Tribunal was created by the Enterprise Act 2002. The current functions of the Tribunal are to hear appeals with respect to decisions made by the Competition and Markets Authority. When a case is heard The Tribunal consists of three members. The panel of chairmen are judges of the Chancery Division of the High Court and other senior lawyers. The ordinary members of the Tribunal have expertise in law, business, accountancy, economics and other related fields. British Airports Authority appealed to the Tribunal following the Competition Commission ruling that it should sell Stansted Airport. The appeal was rejected by the Tribunal in 2011. Subsequently BAA took the case to the Court of Appeal but their appeal has dismissed in 2012. Similarly in 2014 Ryanair was allowed to contest further a Competition Commission order to sell its minority stake in Aer Lingus after the Competition Appeal Tribunal acknowledged that it had raised two important questions that deserved further consideration. Although Ryanair was given leave to take the case to the Court of Appeal the company subsequently lost the case in 2015 when all its grounds for its appeal were rejected.

In September 2009 the OFT fined 103 construction companies £129.5m over allegations of collusion on contract bidding between 2000 and 2006 which then pushed up the price of building contracts. The Competition Appeal Tribunal said the fines were "excessive given the nature of the infringement" and cut them from £41.8m for six companies to just £4.4m. Many experts believed that this judgement cast doubt over how the competition authorities calculate fines.

Question 16.1

(a) Mega mergers in the mobile phone market

Three's proposed takeover of rival O2 is set to be investigated by the UK's competition authorities after the regulator said it threatened choice in Britain's mobile phone market. Hutchison, which already owns Three, has agreed to buy O2 from Spain's Telefonica in a deal worth £10.5bn. The Competition and Markets Authority said the planned acquisition "threatens to affect significantly competition in the UK retail mobile and wholesale mobile markets." BT have also announced the takeover of mobile operator EE in a £12.5bn deal. Rival TalkTalk and Vodafone have already called for competition authorities to step in and to force BT to sell off its Openreach operation.

Investigate how the Competition and Markets Authority and the EU Competition Commission have dealt with these mergers.

http://www.bbc.co.uk/news/business-34471742

http://www.bbc.co.uk/news/business-31144009

(b) Big four auditors face competition probe

Four large companies dominate the audit market- these are firms which audit the accounts of major PLCs. The four companies are Price Waterhouse Coopers, KPMG, Deloitte and Ernst and Young. In 2010 the OFT found that 99% of audit fees paid by the FTSE100 companies went to the big four and between 2002 and 2010 only 2.3% of these companies switched auditor. Between them the major firms audit all but one of Britain's FTSE100 companies and all but ten of the FTSE250. The OFT felt that high entry barriers, high levels of market concentration and an apparent lack of competition justified an investigation by the Competition Commission which the OFT initiated in late 2011.

In 2013 the Competition Commission published a summary of their final package of remedies designed to increase competition within the provision of statutory audit services to major FTSE companies in the UK.

What were the remedies recommended by the Competition Commission?

http://www.iasplus.com/en-gb/news/2013/10/competition-commission-final-audit-remedies

http://www.bbc.co.uk/news/business-24530625

European Union competition policy

The European Union (EU) is becoming increasingly significant with regard to UK competition policy. EU law allows for penalties of up to 10 per cent of turnover, where evidence of anti-competitive behaviour is found. This is the same as in the UK. The EU traditionally left such matters to individual member states, unless there is an appreciable effect on trade between members. Following the **Single European Act (1987)** and the subsequent creation of the single market in 1992, the number of cases covered by this criterion has inevitably increased, with EU investigations in areas such as telecommunications, energy and transport services. Sir Leon Brittan, an EU Commissioner at the time, hailed an agreement, shortly after the Act, to give the EU broader competition policy powers as "unquestionably an historic breakthrough for the EU in the context of the single European market. There can be no internal market without a common competition policy."

The European Union thus has rules to ensure free competition in the Single Market. The **European Commission** is responsible for applying these rules throughout the Community, working closely with national governments. The EU's competition policy was originally set out in Articles 81 and 82 of the Treaty of Rome in 1957 which set up what was then the European Economic Community. Since then the Treaty on the Functioning of the European Union Articles 101 and 102 clarifies in more detail the role, policies and operation of the EU Competition Commission.

Article 87 of the EC Treaty prohibits any aid granted by a member state or through state resources in any form whatsoever which distorts or threatens to distort competition by favouring certain firms or the production of certain goods. The aid in question can take a variety of forms for instance: government grants or interest relief and tax relief.

Article 101 (Article 81) prohibits anti-competitive agreements such as cartels, which may have an appreciable effect on trade between Member States and which prevent, restrict or distort competition in the Single Market. The Commission can grant individual or group exemptions from this prohibition if there are overriding countervailing benefits such as an improvement in efficiency or the promotion of research and development. **Article 102 (Article 82)** prohibits the abuse of a dominant position insofar as it may affect trade between member states. There is no possibility of exemption. Abuse of dominant position was the centrepiece of a long running battle between the EU Competition Commission and Microsoft. The Commission fined Microsoft €497 million because by bundling up Windows Media Player with its Windows operating system Microsoft had damaged rival media players' ability to compete. More recently the European Commission investigated the internet giant Google for allegedly abusing a dominant position. Specifically this involved Google skewing results on its search engine to favour its own price comparison service. This was hotly contested by Google.

The European Commission will consider investigating a merger, which creates a dominant position as a result of which effective competition would be significantly impeded in the Single Market or in a substantial part of it. The Regulation applies to all mergers with a 'Community dimension', defined by reference to turnover criteria.

In 2011 the European Commission blocked a proposed merger between Greece's Olympic Air and Aegean Airlines saying that it would create a "quasi-monopoly". The Commission said the merger would have led to higher fares for four million of the six million Greek and European passengers flying to and from Athens each year. The European Commission also blocked the merger of Ryanair and Aer Lingus in 2007 and again in 2013 arguing it raised "very serious competition problems", in the first ever case of the EU blocking a proposed merger twice. Joaquín Almunia, the then EU competition commissioner, said he had no choice but to block a deal that "would have directly harmed passengers who would have had to pay higher fares as a result." However, in 2015 the European Commission approved the takeover of Aer Lingus by International Airlines Group (IAG) which includes British Airways and Iberia. This was conditional on the release of five daily slot pairs at London-Gatwick airport to facilitate the entry of competing airlines on routes from London to both Dublin and Belfast. In 2016 the European Commission blocked the £10.5bn takeover of O2 by CK Hutchinson, owners of Three mobile, as it was seen as being likely to reduce competition and raise prices in the UK mobile market. The UK regulator Ofcom and the Competition and Markets Authority had already come to the same conclusion in the UK but many eurosceptics felt that this was purely a decision for the UK's regulators, not the EU.

European cross-border mergers and acquisitions have soared in recent years as EU firms seek to compete in an increasingly competitive global market. As trade barriers come down in an enlarged EU, cross-border mergers have become more popular especially as the introduction of the euro has removed currency risks. Recent examples of cross-border mergers have been the acquisition of the Dutch airline KLM by Air France and that of Abbey National by the Spanish bank Santander.

The EU Commission will consider investigating any merger involving worldwide sales greater than €5bn or where EU sales of at least two of the companies exceed €250m. The Commission has the power to bar activities which contravene either **Article 101** or **102** and impose fines on companies it judges to have been at fault to a maximum of 10% of world wide turnover. Many of the changes in UK competition policy introduced by the 1998 Competition Act brought the UK broadly into line with EU competition law.

In 2006 a cartel involving synthetic rubber producers was punished by the Commission, although the 'whistle blower' Bayer was exempt from fines imposed on other cartel members. In 2008 four glass firms were fined a total of €1.38bn for fixing the price of glass used in the automotive industry. Vehicle manufacturers indicated that they might pursue the glass makers, which include the UK based firm Pilkington.

In late 2011 the European Commission fined 11 airlines almost €800m for fixing the price of air cargo between 1999 and 2006. The then EU Competition Commissioner Joaquin Almunia said: "it is deplorable that so many major airlines coordinated their pricing to the detriment of European businesses and European consumers." Air France-KLM were given the biggest fine but Luthansa escaped a fine because it had alerted the regulatory authorities to the existence of the cartel.

Airline	Fine (€)
Air France-KLM (includes Martinair)	339.6m
British Airways	104m
Cargolux	79.9m
Singapore Airlines	74.8m
SAS	70.2m
Cathay Pacific	57.1m
Japan Airlines	35.7m
Air Canada	21.0m
Qantas	8.9m
LAN Chile	8.2m

Source: European Commission

In 2015 the European Commission imposed fines of over €49m on Express Interfracht, part of the Austrian railway Österreichische Bundesbahnen, and Schenker, part of the German railway Deutsche Bahn for operating a cartel in breach of EU competition rules in the market for cargo 'blocktrain' services. Blocktrains make the transport of freight much more efficient by reducing handling and storage costs. The three companies fixed prices and allocated customers for their 'Balkantrain' and 'Soptrain' services in Europe for nearly eight years. EU Competition Commissioner Margrethe Vestager said: "I find it very disappointing that a project to enhance transport efficiency and promote environmentally friendly cargo transport was derailed into a cartel. The European Union needs rail cargo markets to function efficiently on the basis of effective competition and not to be hijacked by vested interests to the detriment of customers."

Source: EU Competition press release

Kühne+Nagel of Switzerland, a large transport and logistics company, also took part in the same cartel but was not fined as it was granted total immunity under the Commission's 2006 leniency notice for revealing

the existence of the cartel. This leniency policy offers companies involved in a cartel – which self-report and hand over evidence – either total immunity from fines or a reduction in the fines that the Commission would have otherwise imposed on them. Express Interfracht and Schenker received reductions in their fines under the leniency notice for cooperating with the investigation. Since all three companies agreed to settle the case with the Commission, their fines were further reduced by 10%. In order to obtain total immunity under the leniency policy, a company which participated in a cartel must be the first one to inform the Commission of an as yet undetected cartel by providing enough information to the Competition Commission to allow it to launch an inspection at the premises of the companies allegedly involved in the cartel.

The European Competition Commission is empowered by the amended **Treaty of Rome** to apply the above Articles and enjoys a number of investigative powers such as inspection of premises and written requests for information. Substantial fines are also at its disposal for violations. Since May 2004 all competition authorities in EU member states are empowered to apply fully the provisions of the Treaty in order to ensure that competition is not distorted or restricted. In order to strengthen the EU's fight against cartels and to speed up investigations a separate cartel directorate has been created within the Commission.

An important issue to consider when a firm or group of firms is being investigated for anti-competitive practices is whether firms should have to prove that they are innocent rather than the competition authorities have to prove their guilt as is the case now, i.e. if you think that you are not abusing your dominant position prove it!

Question 16.2

Google investigated by EU Commission

In 2010, following complaints made by Microsoft, Tripadvisor, Streetmap and others Google was investigated by the EU Commission for possible abuse of dominance. Google accounts for more than 90% of EU-based web searches and it was alleged that the company favours its own products in search engine results.

What were the outcomes of this five year investigation?

http://www.bbc.co.uk/news/technology-32307096
http://www.bbc.co.uk/news/technology-29325580

Question 16.3

Study Figure 16.1 below, which shows how an investigation of a monopoly with significant economies of scale can pose problems for competition authorities when the marginal and average costs of the monopolist (ACm/MCm) is below that of firms in a competitive market (MCc/ACc).

Figure 16.1

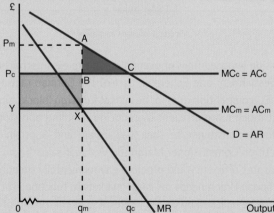

What is the significance of the two shaded areas for the competition authorities?

Unit 17: **The market for corporate control**

The role of shareholders as a discipline on the firm

Shareholders, as the owners of a firm, are risk-takers (i.e. they play part of the role of the entrepreneur – see Unit 1). Having invested in a company by buying its shares, they are entitled to a share of its profits (known as dividends). A second potential source of return on the investment comes in the form of a capital gain. If the company performs well, the price of its shares is likely to increase, allowing shareholders to sell their shares at a profit. However, if the company makes a loss no dividend has to be paid. In the event of the company going bankrupt, shareholders may lose the money they have invested altogether.

As a rule of thumb, there is a correspondence between the level of risk entailed in an investment and its potential return. This provides the basis for the distinction between two types of shareholder. **Preference shareholders** receive a fixed dividend and, if profits are small, are entitled to receive that dividend before any payment is made to ordinary shareholders. Although neither type of shareholder will necessarily receive a dividend if the company makes a loss, preference shareholders will be the first shareholders to get their money back if it goes bankrupt. It is thus clear that the ordinary shareholder faces the greater risk, but if profits are high they will receive a bigger dividend than the preference shareholder.

In theory, a firm will serve the interests of its owners. It is argued that shareholders act as a discipline on the firm because those who run it on a day to day basis, the managers and directors, are ultimately accountable to them (through Annual General Meetings, for example). Accordingly the company will seek to maximise profits and will not be able to be grossly inefficient, because costs must be minimised to this end.

There is not unanimous agreement that this account of the role of shareholders reflects reality. Unit 6 summarises alternative lines of analysis based around the divorce of ownership and control that might result from shareholders not being involved directly with the running of the company.

Even if one accepts that firms act to maximise profits some would argue that the influence of shareholders is not necessarily beneficial from an economic point of view. If shareholders require a rapid return on their investment, this is likely to lead the company to take a short term view of profit maximisation. 'Short termism' may result in companies rejecting investment projects that would deliver a high return in the long run, because the initial expense would entail smaller dividends today. Whether the projects foregone are investment in physical capital or human capital, the effect on the economy is detrimental.

In theory the competition for corporate control of **Public Limited Companies (PLC)** will ensure that long run **shareholder value** is maximised. If profits and dividends fall the market value of the firm's shares will also fall making it easier for the firm to be taken over by a hostile bidder who would quite possibly replace the old management with a new team who would reverse the decline. **The Takeover Panel** looks into pending takeovers from the point of view of shareholder interests while the **Competition and Markets Authority** (Unit 16) uses a wider public interest criterion for its investigations and whether there is a threat to competition.

Sometimes a bid for a PLC is not welcomed by its board of directors and this becomes a **hostile bid** when the bidder appeals directly to the shareholders. In November 2009 UK confectioner Cadbury rejected a £9.8bn ($16.4bn) hostile bid from US food giant Kraft Foods. The Cadbury board said it "emphatically rejected" the offer, which nevertheless had to be put to its shareholders. Kraft offered a mixture of cash and shares for each Cadbury share. "Kraft's offer does not come remotely close to reflecting the true value of our company, and involves the unattractive prospect of the absorption of Cadbury into a low growth conglomerate business model," said the then Cadbury chairman Roger Carr.

However, by February 2010 the three men at the top of Cadbury announced their resignations following Kraft Foods' successful takeover of the chocolate maker. Chairman Roger Carr, chief executive Todd Stitzer

and chief financial officer Andrew Bonfield all left. Kraft sealed its takeover after Cadbury shareholders voted in favour of the deal. Despite the Cadbury board's initial rejection of the hostile bid from Kraft it approved an increased bid of £11.5bn ($18.9bn) and advised shareholders to accept it, saying it offered substantial value for Cadbury shareholders. For many people this takeover was another example of a well established British company falling too easily into the hands of a foreign firm. When a **hostile bid** is launched the board of the takeover target might welcome a 'white knight'. A white knight is a firm that makes a friendly takeover bid for a target company that is facing a hostile takeover.

In 2014 another high profile takeover became a major news story. This time it was in the pharmaceutical sector and involved Pfizer's attempt to buy AstraZeneca, a largely British company. Pfizer, a US drugs company, had several offers rejected by the AstraZeneca board of directors and as it had pledged not to make the bid 'hostile' by appealing directly to the shareholders it ultimately had to withdraw once its final offer had been rejected. Pfizer was bound by the UK Takeover Panel's Takeover Code which meant that when it makes such a pledge to the markets it had to stick to it.

Following the failed Pfizer bid the Takeover Panel strengthened the Takeover Code by requiring a firm to keep its promises following a takeover by providing the Panel with periodic reports on these commitments. The Takeover Panel now has the power to require the appointment of an independent supervisor to assess whether a firm has stuck to its pre-takeover promises. Pfizer had said it would make a series of industrial and investment commitments in the UK for at least five years after the takeover of AstraZeneca in order to ease public concern about the company's motives. Many of these promises made by Pfizer were treated with a good deal of scepticism by analysts and shareholders.

Some firms prefer to remain **private limited companies** rather than have a full listing on the Stock Exchange by becoming a PLC. They prefer to keep a narrower share ownership so that shareholders cannot in their desire for short term returns, disrupt the long term investment plans of a company. Indeed Richard Branson's Virgin group returned to private ownership from PLC status partly for this reason. Many PLC's find that a large number of their shares are owned by institutional investors such as pension funds and insurance companies. These institutions can exert huge influence over the board of a PLC and arguably can exercise too much control over a company. The trend towards private ownership among large firms is quite noticeable and the number of firms with a full listing on the Stock Exchange fell for a time in recent years. Many City analysts blamed this on the complex corporate governance rules which apply to PLC's but not **private limited companies**. However, a listing on the London Stock Exchange is more attractive than a New York listing because of the financial and administrative burden of corporate governance regulations in the United States. In 2012 the UK Government and the then regulator the Financial Services Authority took steps to make it easier for firms to list on the London Stock Exchange.

It is interesting to note that corporate governance can take other forms. For example Network Rail (formerly Railtrack PLC) became in 2002 a company **limited by guarantee**. This meant that they were a private sector organisation and operated as a commercial business but they had no shareholders. Instead Network Rail was accountable to members, who did not receive dividends or share capital. However, Network Rail was reclassified as a government body in 2014 as part of a package of changes to the public finances, which added the company's £30bn debt to UK's national debt. From 1 July 2015 all the members were removed leaving the special member, the Secretary of State for Transport, as the sole member of Network Rail. This made the company essentially part of the Department of Transport answerable to the Secretary of State and Parliament and regulated by the Office of Road and Rail.

Royal Mail Group became a public limited company (plc) in 2001 but it remained wholly owned by the government. This created a more commercially focused company with greater freedom to borrow and at the same time a new regulatory regime was established with an independent regulator. This gave the company commercial freedom without full privatisation, which many felt was necessary but at the time politically sensitive.

With further competitive pressure from private sector firms such as TNT and UK Mail the coalition government (2010-2015) decided to take a radical step in the privatisation of the Royal Mail. The Postal Services Act 2011 allowed for up to 90% of the business to be sold, with a 10% stake for employees. This was by a share sale and took place in 2013. In order to make the company more attractive to investors the assets and liabilities of the Royal Mail pension scheme were taken over by the government. Post Office Ltd (formerly Post Office Counters) provides a wide range of products such as stamps and banking through its network of post office branches. The company was previously a subsidiary of Royal Mail, but is now owned directly by the government and was not part of the privatisation. In 2015 the government raised £591.1m from selling its final stake in Royal Mail at 455p a share. The money was raised from selling a 13% stake in the business, while a 1% stake was awarded to Royal Mail workers. This sale means that the government has received a total of £3.3bn from the Royal Mail privatisation. The 2013 share sale saw the coalition government highly criticised for selling the shares too cheaply. A report found that the shares could have been sold 30p higher than the flotation price.

The credit crunch and subsequent banking crisis in 2008/09 led to increased government holdings in commercial banks such as Lloyds/HBOS and the Royal Bank of Scotland (RBS). With many financial institutions on the brink of collapse the UK government bought sizeable stakes in banks with Northern Rock completely **nationalised**. The UK Government (HM Treasury) still holds a 73% stake in RBS. This stake, as with other government shareholdings in UK banks following the financial crisis, is held and managed through UK Financial Investments Limited, where voting rights as a shareholder are limited to 75% in order for the bank to retain its listing on the London Stock Exchange. In late 2011 it was announced that Virgin Money were going to buy Northern Rock for £747 million, from UK Financial Investments Limited. Although such moves by the government were seen as temporary in response to the crisis it is likely that the state will use its influence to change the way banks are run, in particular how exposed they are to risk and the size of bonuses paid to senior staff. It is also likely that the banking sector will become more tightly regulated both in the UK and globally (see Unit 15).

In addition to reform of the regulatory regime, The Independent Commission on Banking headed by Sir John Vickers issued its report in 2011 which recommended that commercial banks should ring fence their high street retail banking from their high risk investment banking arms. Britain's banks are to be given until 2019 to implement radical reform of their operations to prevent another government rescue of the system. Sir John Vickers said that the reforms would cost between £4bn and £7bn but were more practical and less expensive than the full-scale separation of banks. However, with the enforced mergers of banks during the credit crunch the sector remains highly concentrated and in need of greater competition. Increased competition may possibly come from Tesco and Virgin and other so-called 'challenger banks' in the coming years. The government legislated to implement these proposed banking reforms in the 2013 Banking Reform Act.

The Takeover Panel

While the Competition and Markets Authority are concerned with wider public interest and competition issues the Takeover Panel is concerned with the fair conduct of a takeover bid from the point of view of shareholders when a change in control of companies is possible. The Takeover Panel was set up in 1968 to protect the interests of shareholders of public companies involved in a merger whether they are listed on the Stock Exchange or unlisted. It is concerned with the process of a merger rather than its desirability and is laid down in the City Code on Takeovers and Mergers.

The controversial takeover of Cadbury by Kraft in 2010 raised concerns that UK firms were easy targets for takeover by foreign firms. There was talk of raising the takeover threshold for a successful bid to 75% from 50% approval of the shareholding. The UK Takeover Code was substantially amended in 2011 with a view to addressing the perceived imbalance in UK takeovers between target companies and bidders in hostile situations. The most significant change in the revised Code was to the "put up or shut up" regime. This meant that not only must a prospective bidder now be publicly named in any announcement by the target firm at the beginning of an offer period, but thereafter it now has only 28 days either to launch a bid, or walk away and be prevented from making an offer for at least six months. Bidders must also reveal details of their financing and advisory fees. Following Pfizer's attempt to buy Astra Zeneca in 2014 issues regarding post offer promises by the bidding company led to further amendments to the Takeover Code in 2015.

The role of the Stock Exchange

The Stock Exchange provides a market mechanism for the exchange of second hand shares. Far fewer people would buy new shares in a company if there were no market to sell them on if they needed to sell at short notice. This is very important given the importance of new share issues for companies needing finance for new investment.

The existence of this mechanism provides a second discipline on the firm: the threat of hostile takeover bids. An inefficient company is likely to be subject to takeover attempts, because the inefficiency leads to it under-performing in terms of profits and this is likely to be reflected in its share price. This low share price makes the company an attractive proposition for predators who believe they can run the company more efficiently. Equally if a firm has a high price earnings ratio (P/E ratio) it may be attractive to buyers because its high current share price relative to low past earnings indicates promising future prospects.

It was argued above that the influence of shareholders might in fact damage the long run interests of the firm and the wider economy. Parallel arguments can be constructed with regard to the Stock Exchange and the threat of takeover. These may contribute to short termism as firms act to fend off hostile bids. In an attempt to do so, they may launch a drive for high short term profits, forsaking potentially profitable investment projects in the interests of paying higher dividends to keep the shareholders happy. This could lead to a loss of dynamic efficiency as investment falls.

Further, some takeover bids are not based upon any perceived inefficiency in the company taken over. Horizontal integration (Unit 3), for example, results in greater market concentration and affords the newly combined firm greater control of its market. This might allow it to exploit consumers in the interests of increasing profit levels.

Question 17.1

(a) Explain the statement that "the shareholder plays part of the role of the entrepreneur".

(b) The exchange of shares is somewhat speculative in nature. One is likely to invest in a company if one expects its share price to rise, in the hope of making a capital gain. Explain the statement that "expectations of changes in share prices are self-fulfilling".

(c) Give three reasons why an individual might buy shares in a company quoted on the Stock Exchange.

Question 17.2

Private equity firms acquire control or a significant minority holding in a firm and then look to maximise the value of that investment. Boots the Chemist (Alliance Boots) was a public limited company (PLC) listed on the Stock Exchange but in 2007 it was bought out in a private equity transaction by KKR & Co. L.P. In June 2012, Walgreens the US owned retail pharmacist bought a 45% stake in Alliance Boots and then bought the remaining 55% stake from KKR in 2015.

Investigate the role of private equity groups in relation to the corporate control of UK firms.

Question 17.3

A sovereign wealth fund is a state-owned investment fund comprised of financial assets such as shares, government bonds, and property. 'Surplus' countries in the Middle and Far East are the most likely nations to be operating sovereign wealth funds.

Investigate the importance of sovereign wealth funds in the ownership of UK firms.

Unit 18: Government policy towards the private sector

In recent years governments have wished to increase the role of the private sector in activities previously the sole preserve of the public sector, because they believe that this is conducive to the efficient use of economic resources. **Privatisation** is one example (see Unit 15); another is the **Private Finance Initiative (PFI)**, encouraging private investment in projects that once would have been state funded. **Public Private Partnerships (PPP)** is the umbrella name given to a range of initiatives which involve the private sector in the operation of public services, the PFI is the most widely used initiative.

The Private Finance Initiative (PFI)

Until relatively recently it was widely accepted that certain services, such as hospitals and prisons, should not only be delivered by the public sector, but also produced or provided by it. The PFI challenges this supposition, and successive governments believed that private sector finance and management expertise, combined with the profit incentive, enabled the private sector to produce services more cheaply than the public sector ever could.

In the majority of cases, the PFI had involved the designing, financing, building and operation of capital assets such as hospitals and schools by the private sector. The private sector then secures a return on its investment in one of two ways. For some schemes, such as toll roads and bridges, the general public is charged as and when they use the facility. Examples include privately financed prisons where the public sector pays for the availability of prison cells. The north Birmingham relief road now called the 'M6 toll' is a high profile example of a PFI project in action where the user pays directly for the service provided to Midland Expressway Ltd who have a 50 year contract to operate the road. For others, the public sector is charged for the provision within the terms of the contact. Although the terms of PFI contracts vary a hospital built using the scheme would normally mean the NHS Trust paying an annual fee once the building is operational. This would be for possibly 30 years. Within the hospital the cleaning, maintenance and catering would be provided by firms within the PFI consortium leaving the medical staff to carry out the clinical services. In theory a new hospital is provided without a large immediate burden on the taxpayer and the medical teams concentrate on their areas of expertise leaving ancillary services to the PFI consortium.

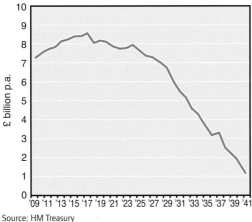

Figure 18.1: The cost of PFI, projected payments 2009-10 to 2040-41 (£bn p.a.)

Source: HM Treasury

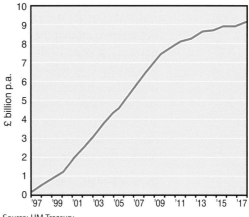

Figure 18.2: The cost of PFI, payments under PFI contracts 1997-98 to 2017-18 (£bn p.a.)

Source: HM Treasury

A limited number of PFI projects are funded by public private partnerships (PPP), although overall control of the project rests with the private sector. The public sector contribution is usually made to secure the wider social benefits (for example, road de-congestion) of a project that might not otherwise have gone ahead. The London Underground's investment programme was an example of PPP. Under the scheme, two engineering consortiums, Metronet and Tube Lines, won 30-year contracts worth £17bn to modernise the

The London Underground's investment programme was an example of PPP.

tracks, stations and tunnels, thereby splitting the tube's infrastructure from its operation, by London Underground. The private sector was to pay 25% towards the work, government grants 60% and fares 15%. However, the contract was so complex that it cost the taxpayer £455m in lawyers' and consultants' expenses just to draw it up! The deals were performance-related, so the companies were rewarded according to their success in reducing service delays. However since 2008 the underground network has been maintained by Transport for London (a public sector body), after Metronet went into administration. The whole 30 year project was plagued by delays and overspends as well as controversy over just how much better the tube network had become under Metronet's upgrade programme. Some blamed Metronet's shareholders for the collapse of the PPP arrangement but it had cost taxpayers £2bn.

Numerous doubts have been expressed for several years about whether the theoretical benefits of the PFI can be delivered in practice. These include the possibility that high administration and costs, added to the fact that currently it is more expensive for the private sector to borrow than for the public sector, prevent PFI schemes making the planned cost savings. The public sector's borrowing costs are closely related to government bond yields while private sector firms borrow at higher market rates. Also, there are worries that private firms reduce the quality of buildings and services in order to reduce cost. There are, however, levels of service specified in contracts and the firms are penalised if these are not met. In certain PFI prison contracts the government receives £100,000 for every escaped prisoner! Perhaps the chief benefit of the scheme is that the risk of capital projects costing more than anticipated is no longer borne by the tax-payer. It is common for the cost of a project to escalate while it is in progress. If this happens during a PFI scheme, the private sector must meet the cost.

In recent years almost all new NHS hospitals and many state schools and prisons have been built with private-sector money. Most of the contracts last for about 25 years, with the Government paying for the buildings in stages. During the contract private firms are required to maintain the buildings to a high standard and keep them clean. Once the contract expires the building reverts to public sector ownership.

But Public Private Partnerships (PPPs), such as **contracting out** ancillary services to private firms, to taking over the management of a school, have been vigorously opposed by the trade unions. They say that public-sector staff who are transferred to the private sector have to work for less pay and in worse conditions. The PFI helps to reduce the level of government debt because borrowing by private companies under the scheme is not counted as government debt – off balance sheet. This poses a possible problem that the PFI is often preferred even when it is not the best option.

In October 2005 Britain's biggest Trade Union (Unison) demanded in its report 'A House Built on Sand' that the PFI be scrapped as the research that had been used to promote it was biased and manipulated. The then Labour government argued that although the PFI costs more in terms of building costs, it delivered value because it avoids overruns more than non-PFI work.

The poor state of the UK's public sector assets after years of under-investment had to be addressed. The alternative to PFI was higher government borrowing or increased taxation. This is an unpalatable alternative for those in government trying to improve the standard of the UK's public services.

In the recent recession many PFI schemes encountered funding crises from construction companies and banks which form the consortiums which finance the projects. Work on schools, hospitals and road widening programmes were delayed. Vince Cable, a long-time sceptic of PFI, said in 2009 that the government should go back to more traditional public financing structures rather than use taxpayers' money to prop up the public-private model. "We need to be very careful about the taxpayer taking all the risks and the private partners taking all the benefits."

When the coalition government was elected in 2010 there was a major re-think asking whether the PFI was in reality a very expensive way of providing much needed capital assets. Clearly some of the terms of PFI contracts were unfavourable with alarming examples of over-charging the public sector. Examples include a bill of £963 to install an aerial in the consultant's common room in a hospital. Further areas of apparent poor value for money include the M25 road-widening project plus a number of Ministry of Defence contracts such as Air Tanker re-fuelling. Equally worrying for many is the selling of PFI equity in many of the 700 hospitals, schools and prisons that have been built under the scheme. If PFI is so lucrative to investors then the taxpayer is, according to some, losing out when it comes to value for money. In 2012 Peterborough City Hospital, built under a PFI scheme, was given a £46m bail-out little more than a year after it opened. The hospital is tens of millions of pounds in debt and has to pay the PFI consortium £3m per month as part of its contract. The 'FiReControl' project was designed to upgrade fire and rescue to nine regional control centres in England instead of 46 local control rooms. However the project was cancelled after problems with the IT system. The cost of this PFI project has reached £270m with rent, maintenance, water and electricity bills costing over £1m per month. Many of the buildings stand empty.

Consort Healthcare Limited built the Royal Blackburn Hospital in 2006 at a cost of £109m, and will receive £796m from the East Lancashire Hospitals NHS Trust over 36 years. The deal includes other services, such as maintenance, security, window cleaning, and pest control. A construction project at Burnley General Hospital, which saw £30m spent there, involved a contract with SPC Ltd Facilities Management. The same trust will have to pay back £181m over 35 years, with the deal including security and car parking services. These financial commitments are a huge strain on already stretched budgets and East Lancashire is looking into trying to buy itself out of these contracts. Northumbria Healthcare NHS Foundation Trust borrowed money from the local council to buy itself out of PFI contracts in order to save significant sums in future payments. NHS Trusts owe £80bn in PFI loan repayments and 'unitary charges', which are the ongoing running costs of maintaining PFI hospitals. NHS Trusts will make about £2bn in PFI repayments a year and have first claim on a Trust's budget before money is spent on clinical services.

The controversy surrounding PFI schemes led to the Chancellor George Osborne announcing an overhaul of PFI in 2013. The new initiative called PF2 was designed to ensure taxpayers shared in the rewards as well as the risks of these schemes, firstly by making the government a shareholder, and secondly by introducing more transparent assessments of value for money compared with traditional public sector financing. However few schemes have yet to be signed off under PF2. Only one hospital has decided to use the new model, while plans to use it for military housing were dropped. In addition an attempt to use PF2 for the schools refurbishment programme were delayed. PFI is a huge financial millstone round the neck of many public services and UK taxpayers now owe £305bn in PFI repayments across over 700 projects for the next 30 years (see Figures 18.1 and 18.2).

As a result of Quantitative Easing long term interest rates are very low and ironically it is now very cheap for governments to borrow to finance big capital projects. Despite the recent commitment to deficit reduction, borrowing to finance the building of 'social capital' such as roads and schools is not seen by many as a fiscal problem. These assets as part capital spending can be used for many years by future generations.

Contracting out

Communities around the world have in some cases improved quality and lowered cost by **contracting out** local services. Under this scheme in the UK, local authorities such as county and district councils act as enabling authorities that assess local needs and then specify the service they require. Bids are invited from in-house teams, voluntary organisations and private sector contractors. The emphasis shifts from the local council as a monopoly provider and manager, to the council as enabler and monitor of high standards. In theory the introduction of competition drives down costs, encourages innovation and improves standards. In the UK local authorities have contracted out to private firms such services as household rubbish collection, home support services and office catering. Although free marketers will support the idea of resources no longer being directed by 'the dead hand of the state' there is extensive evidence that lower costs are achieved by lower wages for staff accompanied by poorer terms of employment and inferior working conditions.

The process of awarding these contracts for local authority services was originally organised through **compulsory competitive tendering**. This was introduced in the 1980s, and local authorities were forced to open up in-house services, such as refuse collection and road maintenance, to private competition in order to effort to reduce costs and improve value for money. Compulsory competitive tendering was never popular because many believed that it placed too much emphasis on cutting costs at the expense of quality of service. Since 2000 compulsory competitive tendering has largely been replaced by what is called '**best value**'. Best value requires local authorities to deliver a continuous improvement in the standard and efficiency of their services, bringing in outside private firms where it is seen appropriate. **Competitive tendering** is still used by local authorities as evidenced by this quote from the Bracknell Forest Homes web site regarding the employment of an electrical contractor to complete the digital switchover for council houses in the area: "Bracknell Forest Homes has used a competitive tender process to select an experienced, qualified and best value contractor to do the installation work." Competitive tendering is also used for franchises on the various routes on the rail network e.g. the West Coast Line.

Best value is defined as: "a system securing continuous improvement in the exercise of all functions undertaken by a public authority, whether statutory or not, having regard to a combination of economy, efficiency and effectiveness." Best value pledges to provide genuine value for money for the public sector. It intends to deliver target-driven results in public services which will be quality-benchmarked rather than price benchmarked and subject to external controls.

According to Chris Bovis in his article 'Replacing Compulsory Competitive Tendering with Best Value' – "The best value initiative can be seen as a genuine attempt to improve the delivery and increase the quality of public services local authorities and other public bodies deliver. It is a moderate and non-confrontational system which is based upon a balance between quality and price of public services. Best value would result in best procurement practice for public services by elevating public consultation and quality benchmarking as requisite criteria for genuine value for money in the delivery of public services."

Nationalisation

Over the last thirty years nationalisation, the process of taking a private industry or private assets into public ownership by the state, has been off the political agenda. Successive governments of different political persuasions have been more interested in the reverse process of privatisation. Nationalisation was a major policy of the post war Labour government (1945-51) when railways, electricity, gas and the coal industry were among key 'strategic' sectors that were nationalised. Throughout the 1950s and 60s and 70s these industries remained in the public sector and the process went further with the nationalising of the steel industry in 1967, British Leyland in 1974 and aerospace and shipbuilding in 1977. By the late 1970s, the nationalised industries accounted for 10pc of Britain's GDP, 14pc of investment and 8pc of employment. These nationalised industries were run by boards of directors appointed by government ministers and thus these board members were answerable to politicians and Parliament. Their finances were controlled by the government. Many firms in the nationalised sector made losses (rail and coal for example) while others made disappointing levels of profits as well as being plagued by low productivity and poor industrial relations. However, they were subject to unwanted political interference from ministers often looking only to the short term and they also suffered a chronic lack of new investment.

The privatisation programme of the 1980s and 90s under the Conservative governments of Margaret Thatcher and John Major transferred nearly all the major nationalised firms into private sector ownership as PLCs although many were subject to regulation (see Unit 15). The most recent major privatisation was the Royal Mail, which was completed in 2015. The only major policy moves in the reverse direction in recent years have been driven by crises – Railtrack PLC was nationalised in 2002, and in 2008 a number of UK banks became effectively government owned because they required massive injections of cash during the financial crisis. The government bought significant shareholdings in banks such as RBS and Lloyds although they retained their PLC status, and over time the government shareholding has been steadily reduced. One of the rail franchises, East Coast Mainline was in the hands of Directly Operated Railways, a subsidiary of the Department for Transport from 2009 to 2015. The government took control of the franchise when its previous operator National Express ran into financial difficulties. In 2015 a joint venture involving Virgin and Stagecoach took control of the train services from the public sector.

Since the election of Jeremy Corbyn as the leader of the Labour Party in 2015 nationalisation has emerged again as possible policy of a major political party with the railways and the energy sector as candidates for state ownership. The railways are already part state owned as Network Rail is a part of the Department for Transport but the franchises held by train operating companies such as Virgin and Stagecoach are privately operated. If nationalisation did occur it could be done relatively cheaply by the government taking over the franchises as each ran out. This would take several years as some have over ten years left to run, but using this patient method of nationalisation, the railways could operate as a state owned monopoly by 2030 with minimal public expenditure. Many transport experts believe that rail was a flawed privatisation with the fragmentation of the old British Rail leading to a loss of the benefits of a natural monopoly. It has always seemed odd to many that the track and signals is run separately (by Network Rail) to the train services operating on this infrastructure (Virgin and Stagecoach).

The renationalisation of the energy industry would be a more complex affair. It could cost as much as £185bn to bring the energy industry back under state control through the traditional method of nationalisation, that is buying the industry at its current market value. This is not possible with the levels of government debt and the commitment of both political parties to reduce the fiscal (budget) deficit. There has also been suggestions that EU treaties and directives prohibit the renationalisation of the energy sector. Better regulation of the sector and increased incentives for new entrants may be a better and cheaper option for the gas and electricity sectors.

Government failure

Government failure occurs when government intervention, maybe to correct a market failure, has the effect of introducing a market distortion which causes allocative inefficiency. It is often assumed that once market failure has been identified it can be either reduced or eliminated through government intervention, for example, by imposing taxes, controls and regulation. This benign view of the role of the government in the economy centring on the use of public policy to correct market failure wherever it is found to exist illustrates what may be called the **public interest theory** of government behaviour. This theory argues that governments intervene in a benevolent fashion in the economy in order to eliminate waste and to achieve an efficient and socially desirable allocation of resources.

Public choice theory, however, looks at political decisions from the point of view of self-seeking or utility maximising politicians. If politicians are assumed to want to maximise their utility by maximising votes then they will not be very interested in the welfare of those who do not vote. If we assume that they wish to

maximise the number of seats they win in the House of Commons, then they will be much more interested in the welfare of those in the marginal constituencies than those in the seats that never change hands. As soon as we admit that public choice theory is plausible, we have to admit that even a government with the correct information might reduce society's welfare when intervening in the market. For example, subsidies may prevent the exit of a firm from an industry, but preserve employment in a marginal parliamentary constituency.

Darker versions of public choice theory are possible and are sadly all too applicable to some countries. If we assume politicians have the objective of making money, then they will make decisions according to the highest bribe on offer. Governments take resources away from taxpayers and reallocate them. Any re-allocation of resources influenced by bribery is likely to be a very long way from welfare maximising from society's viewpoint.

Government failure can occur through the over-taxing of demerit goods and negative exter-nalities, and through the over-provision of public and merit goods. Heavy taxation of

Heavy taxation of cigarettes has led to many people in the South-East of England taking a short ferry trip to France or Belgium to buy cheap cigarettes.

cigarettes has led to many people in the South-East of England taking a short ferry trip to France or Belgium to buy cheap cigarettes some of which are sold on to friends. High tax on petrol in Northern Ireland has led in the past to many people crossing the border into the Republic of Ireland to fill their tanks. This can be related to the 'law of unintended consequences' when a government policy (tax, regulation or subsidy) has an effect which is unanticipated. Would the government have banned smoking in public places if they had known how much it would have accelerated the decline of the pub trade with tens of pubs closing every week? Probably yes, but there would have been a few misgivings.

In 1994 the government introduced Air Passenger Duty which is charged on the carriage of passengers flying from a UK airport. It is imposed on the airlines but is usually passed on in its entirety to passengers. The tax is designed to cut emissions by reducing the number of flights but anecdotal evidence suggests that Air Passenger Duty has actually increased emissions because long haul travellers in order to avoid the tax are drawn towards taking connecting flights via non-UK airports in Europe rather than flying direct.

Many economists believe that some of the privatisations carried out in the 1980s and 1990s produced badly structured industries which have led to significant difficulties in recent years. This could arguably apply to the energy sector and the railways which are both large complex industries which may have been privatised more effectively using a different model. Regulation is made more difficult and government intervention has been significant in recent years as both sectors have faced major challenges. There is also an additional issue regarding ownership – should the UK government have allowed much of our water, energy and transport providers to fall into foreign ownership? Regulatory capture occurs when a regulatory body such as Ofwat and Ofgem appear to operate in favour of the vested interests of producers rather than consumers. It could be argued that regulators can often prevent the market operating freely. In many cases regulators may have insufficient information to adequately balance the interest of consumers, producers and investors and thus inevitably the result of regulation is flawed resulting in inefficient outcomes.

Government action does not have to lead to government failure. The most prosperous countries in the world generally have a large proportion of their GDP – anything from 30% to 50% – allocated by the public sector. Vast amounts of resources are allocated by governmental decision, often to deal with the perceived failure of the market to provide appropriate quantities of important goods and services. If governments sometimes make mistakes, that is not a good reason for pessimism and cynicism.

The UK government spends almost £140bn on health care as it is perceived to be a merit good producing significant external benefits from consumption. NHS care is free at point of consumption with a 100% subsidy but it can be argued that this can itself lead to government failure. In the diagram below there is under consumption of health care when it is provided by the market at q where MPB = MPC. Thus there is a potential welfare gain if health care is subsidised so that the consumption of health care is at the socially optimal level at q1 where MSC = MSB. The lower price of health care would increase quantity demanded to the socially optimal level.

Figure 18.3

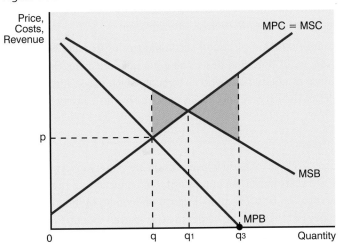

However, in the UK there is a 100% subsidy for health care making it free which increases quantity demanded to the point where MPB touches the quantity axis at q3. This results in a welfare loss and as the welfare loss exceeds the potential welfare there is government failure. How can this be? Free at point of consumption health care produces excess demand where some 'patients' at GP surgeries or A&E departments present themselves with minor conditions that could be self-treated possibly via a visit to the chemist. Overburdened health services mean that genuine patients get poorer treatment or people are misdiagnosed as the pressure on the service mounts. Free health care raises the issue of moral hazard when people abuse their bodies via excess drinking, smoking or eating, knowing that their treatment will be free on the NHS. How much do patients value their health care when they do not pay for it directly? It could thus be argued that the overburdened NHS is showing the symptoms of government failure.

Question 18.1

What are the advantages and disadvantages of nationalising key UK industries such as railways, energy and telecommunications?

Question 18.2

What is PF2?
PF2 was announced in George Osborne's autumn statement of 2012 and followed a critical enquiry into PFI. During the review all PFIs in development were halted. It is effectively a rebranding of the PFI. It aims to draw new investors into the market by further limiting their financial exposure and giving still greater responsibility for risk to the public sector.

(Continued overleaf)

Key features of PF2 are:

- Soft Facilities Management is no longer part of the contract but is procured separately by the Hospital Trust.

- Equity investment in the project will form 20-29% of the total financing, compared with between 10 and 15% in the PFI contracts.

- Of that equity investment, the government will itself hold between 30-49% making it a minority investor and taking on both the risk and profit of that role.

- Public sector equity investment will be arranged through a new unit in the Treasury – Infrastructure UK described as a 'commercially-focused unit located in the Treasury separate from the procuring authority to make 'commercial decisions'.

- An SPV through which the equity finance in channelled will have Treasury representation on the Board but not local authority or NHS Trust representation.

- Limited transparency remains, although according to the Treasury website it provides more details of the progress of financing deals, these are uninformative; there is not greater transparency for instance of equity transactions, through which major additional profits have been secured under PFI and which were specifically criticized by the Treasury Select Committee review.

Is PF2 any better?

The answer generally is no.

Public sector costs are likely to increase because of greater equity investment by the government (and equity investment costs more than borrowing). The annual return that equity investors expect is 12-15% compared to the 6 to 7% annual return on lending by financial institutions such as banks. Value for money will therefore be harder to achieve even though PF2s will have more equity and therefore will be thought to be lower risk.

The PF2 is an example of increasingly complex ways of financing projects. Bond finance is likely to become more common, as well as greater pension fund, insurance company and other financial institution investment in PF2 projects. As this trend gathers pace, *political control of planning and procurement processes will become more inaccessible and problematic.*

As Dexter Whitfield, Director of the European Services Strategy Unit, has said, the PF2 programme has to be ended and replaced by a programme of public investment, while "New regulatory controls on existing projects should require democratic accountability, rigorous contract monitoring, new disclosure requirements and a ban on the transfer of ownership of infrastructure assets to offshore tax havens."

In July 2014 the Treasury announced approval for £353m Midland Metropolitan Hospital financed under PF2, which includes £100m from public dividend capital to make the project affordable. Other new hospitals currently in the pipeline appear to be using a hybrid form of PFI and PF2 financing. The Royal Liverpool and Broadgreen University Hospital is a £429m project for a 664 bed, single rooms only hospital. It is to be funded using £118m of the Trust's own money, £94m public dividend capital, £128m from a PFI and an expected £89m from the European Investment Bank.

Source: http://www.dropnhsdebt.org.uk/

Using the article and the BBC Panorama programme of a few years ago (https://www.youtube.com/watch?v=32AglebZSZQ) assess the extent to which PFI is a better option than the public sector when financing facilities such as the building of new hospitals and the running of non-medical services within them.